THE MOBIUS GUIDES

chakras

THE MOBIUS GUIDES

chakras

NAOMI OZANIEC

First published in Great Britain in 2003 by Hodder and Stoughton
A division of Hodder Headline

A Mobius paperback

1 3 5 7 9 10 8 6 4 2

A CIP catalogue record for this title is available from the British Library

ISBN 0 340828013

Typeset in Fairfield Light by
Palimpsest Book Production Limited, Polmont, Stirlingshire
Printed and bound in Great Britain by
Mackays of Chatham Ltd, Chatham, Kent

Hodder and Stoughton
A division of Hodder Headline
338 Euston Road
London NW1 3BH

contents

introduction

Know Thyself

Delphic Injunction

This book is presented as a guide for beginners. Yet we should not disguise the fact that the subject matter is complex. Indeed knowledge of the chakras was once handed on only from teacher to student through a closely guarded secret tradition. The secrecy was intended to ensure that this sacred knowledge was not abused. The closed environment of the ashram or spiritual retreat provided a safe atmosphere in which the unfolding soul might be nourished. The holders of the tradition were fully aware that spiritual growth brings its own dynamics. We need to admit at the outset that there is no substitute for the spiritual teacher whose wide experience and warm heart take the student into the tradition slowly and with care. Nor is there any substitute for personal experience. Awakening is never a matter of detached intellectual musing but a total and fully encompassing encounter of heart, mind, body and soul. Only such intense experiences have the power to break into a new level of being.

In the West, sacred knowledge is now freely available. The ashram has been superseded by the workshop. The impetus for the dissemination of teaching has moved from the tradition holders to those who seek metaphysical knowledge. Our spiritual hunger is a sign of the times. We should not, however, confuse information about spiritual awakening with the process itself. Ideally the one is but a preparation for the other. Nevertheless information has its place.

This book can be no more than an introduction to a vast subject. It will awaken you only through gentle but probing questions and guided meditations. It will initiate you into the complexity and importance of the subject, but it does not seek to be more than an overview. However, perhaps this little book will awaken you to deep questions and puzzling relationships. If so, it will have served its purpose, for a journey of a thousand miles begins with a single step.

Living Energies

These flowers are the sense organs of the soul.

Rudolf Steiner

Many words of Indian origin have passed into the English language. The Sanskrit word *chakra* is now appearing in our vocabulary. It simply means 'wheel'. This symbolism tells us a great deal. The wheel is circular in shape and turns upon its axis. Each chakra is also described as a lotus, *padma*. The lotus, much like a lily, is an extremely beautiful flower with many petals. The chakra is similar to both the wheel and the lotus as it revolves around the centre and unfolds its individual vortices.

It is clear that we are in the realm of the symbolic and the metaphysical, for by tradition we are using the language of analogy and metaphor, which is always the expansive vocabulary of spiritual experience. We may define the chakra as an energy centre which spins like a wheel and opens like a flower. Metaphysical concepts, however, do not belong purely to the world of spiritual experience; scientific enquiry has in many cases confirmed age-old beliefs.

Dr Hiroshi Motoyama bridges the world of the scientific and the spiritual with dual authority. He is both a scientist and a Shinto priest. Motoyama is the founder of the International Association for Religion and Parapsychology. In 1974 he was recognised by UNESCO as one of the world's ten foremost parapsychologists. He is especially interested to verify scientifically the claims put forward by proponents of spiritual practices. Several significant experiments have been conducted under his auspices.

He has specifically developed a Chakra Instrument which is designed to detect minute electrical, magnetic and optical changes which occur in the immediate environment of the experimental subject. In a typical experimental situation, the subject sat in an electrostatically secure room which was internally lined with aluminium sheeting and shielded by lead sheeting embedded in the walls. A round copper electrode and photo-electro cell were placed in front of the body, level with the location of a supposed chakra. During one test on the centres of the stomach and heart, the subject was monitored for a period of three minutes at each of the two locations. Separate readings were taken one minute before a state of concentration, during concentration, and one minute after concentration.

Curiously, when an advanced yoga practitioner was tested, the two centres gave quite different results. The stomach centre showed no change in measurable activity during the three-minute monitoring period. However, the heart centre showed a considerable intensification of measurable activity during the period of concentration. This difference corresponded to the subject's regular spiritual practice. He regularly meditated on the heart centre during meditation. The subject did not as a rule use the solar plexus as a focal point for meditation as he suffered from a serious digestive disorder.

When working with another subject, Motoyama found that the increased activity of the heart chakra was sufficient to produce a measurable effect which was detected by the photoelectric cell. In other words the activity of the heart chakra was enough to produce a weak but measurable physical light. Moreover the subject was asked to press a button whenever she thought that she experienced the emission of psi-energy. The subjective feelings corresponded to the objectively measured periods of activity. It was experiments like these which were conducted with 100 subjects which led Motoyama to conclude 'that mental concentration on a chakra activates it'.[1]

Additionally, as an advanced yoga practitioner, Motoyama has himself experienced an awakening within each of the chakras. In the spirit of scientific enquiry he has recorded all his experiences with the detachment of the trained mind. Such reports are invaluable guides to those seeking to understand the dynamics of this path.

Such findings and experiences take us deeply into the relationships between energy and matter. Spiritual traditions have long believed that all matter produces an energy field. The existence of such life-fields was once a matter of metaphysical speculation. However, twentieth-century developments have belatedly confirmed what spiritual teachers have taught down the ages. There can be little doubt now of the existence of an energy field, now suitably dignified with twentieth-century terminology: the L Field, bioplasma, the LEF, the Living Energy Field. Kirlian photography has revealed the subtle body of plant, vegetable, tree, animal and human alike.

If a fresh thistle leaf (see photo overleaf) has its own luminescence is it really too difficult to believe in the human aura, the Living Energy Field? Unlike a thistle leaf, the human is complex and sophisticated, with specialised biological systems. Simple cell structures produce a generalised energy field. The human being produces a complex and specialised energy field, a living network of subtle energies. The chakras are significant centres within this living network. The channels which make up this network are often likened to rivers. Like rivers these lines of energy may be blocked by obstruction, drained empty, full and nourishing. Where many rivers meet, a confluence is formed. It is a powerful pooling of energies, a whirling vortex of force. This is a chakra: the confluence where life energies meet. It is the wheel of life.

There are seven major chakras. They are located at the base of the spine, at the reproductive centre, at the solar plexus, the heart, the throat, the brow and finally at the crown of the head. These sites in turn represent the body's major systems: excretion, reproduction, digestion, circulation, respiration and the complex functions of cognition. The crown chakra is sometimes regarded as a unique centre of consciousness and not counted with the first six chakras. It is important to remember that there are other minor centres also, so numbering systems can sometimes appear to be different. (See Figure 1)

The Eastern titles given to the chakras throws more light on their individual functions. The first or base chakra is called the *Muladhara* chakra. Muladhara means root. Like a tree we need to be firmly rooted in the physical world. The second chakra is called the *Svadisthana* chakra. Svadisthana means 'sweetness' or 'one's own abode'. Both titles reflect the intimate function of this chakra. Violation at this level of being is indeed a total violation of 'one's own abode'. The third chakra is called the *Manipura* chakra. This name means 'lustrous gem', or 'city of jewels'. The solar plexus chakra is a storehouse of subtle energy. This centre should glow and radiate like a shining gem or bowl of jewels piled high. The fourth, the heart chakra, is called the *Anahata* chakra. This name means 'unstruck'. It refers to a sound that is heard but not struck, a subtle reference to the more sensitised qualities of this chakra. Only a sensitised ear hears a delicate note. The fifth, the throat chakra, is called the *Vishuddi* chakra. Vishuddi means 'to purify'. The process of purification selects out impurities and collects a refined essence. This chakra demands that we use the power of speech and communication to distinguish between those words and thoughts which are allied to a purpose and those which are no more than meaningless noise. The sixth, the brow chakra, is called the *Ajna* chakra. 'Ajna' means 'to know'. This chakra refers to the function of immediate and direct insight which transcends the limitations of deductive thought. The seventh chakra, at the crown of the head, is called the *Sahasrara* chakra. This name means 'thousandfold'. This chakra is shown as an open lotus with a thousand petals. The Sahasrara chakra symbolises the idea that a human being has a thousand qualities to unfold. In other words the qualities dormant within the human being are without number. This sevenfold pattern is the blueprint for the human being. We are truly made in the image of the divine. As we unfold this blueprint, we become ourselves, we become human.

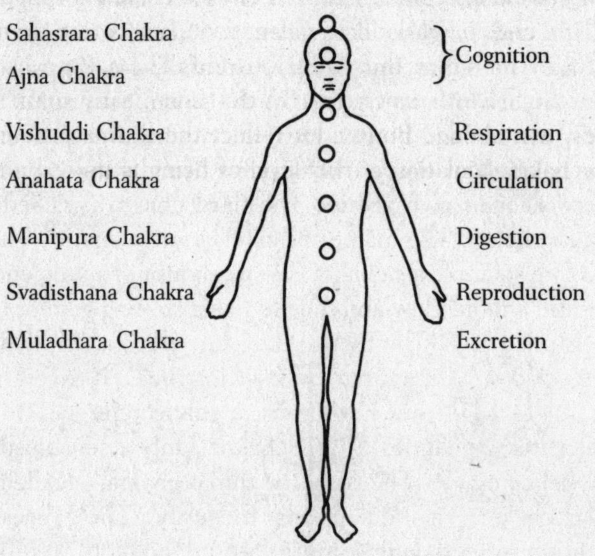

Figure 1 *Chakras and physical systems*

Subtle anatomy

The time has come however when the fact that there is an energy body underlying the nervous system must be recognised by the world at large, and when the nature of the seven centres, their structures and location should be grasped technically, and when the laws of their unfoldment should be widely known.

The Tibetan

All matter produces a subtle counterpart. The physical system produces a subtle body. The living network of nerves has a subtle counterpart, a network of subtle currents which permeate the whole being. The chakras are an integral part of this system. Acupuncture recognises 14 major meridians. More esoteric systems emphasise three major psychic meridians: Ida,

Pingala and Sushumna. Sushumna rises vertically through the spine. Ida and Pingala, also called the Ganges and Yamuna rivers, are the lunar and solar currents. Ida, Pingala and Sushumna each rise at the base of the spine. Sushumna rises vertically but Ida and Pingala cross and return over the central current creating an image that is symbolised by the caduceus, the wand of Hermes. (See Figures 2 and 3.)

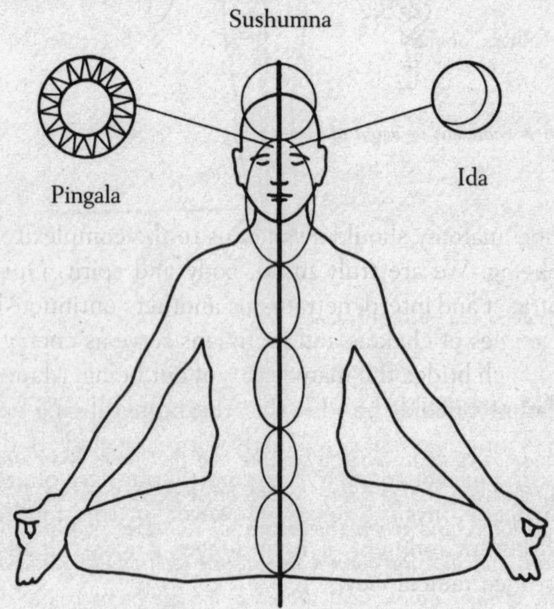

Figure 2 *Subtle energies*

Figure 3 *The caduceus or wand of Hermes*

The subtle anatomy should awaken us to the complexity of the human being. We are truly mind, body and spirit. Our many levels interact and interpenetrate one another continuously. The subtle energies of chakras and meridians serve as energy transformers which bridge the many levels of our being. Many spiritual traditions uphold the idea that the human being operates through a number of increasingly more refined 'bodies' or vehicles of consciousness. We are mostly unaware of anything other than our physical selves. However, in this increasingly spiritualised environment, it is no longer so difficult to entertain this once radical view.

The chakras themselves are multi-levelled, as we are. Each chakra may potentially function at seven levels. By analogy we may think of each chakra as a radio which may be tuned to different frequencies. We so infrequently 'reset' ourselves to anything other than a purely physical wavelength that we find it difficult to comprehend the reality of other states of experience. Yet many travellers have found the path of higher vibrations and have recorded their journeys for those seeking to walk the same path.

Awakening to Life

I longed to attain the condition of consciousness, said to be the ultimate goal of Yoga, which carries the embodied spirit to regions of unspeakable glory and bliss.

Gopi Krishna

It is clear that the entire subtle anatomy system, which includes the seven major chakras, is simply not visible to the naked eye. We do not see electricity or magnetism either, yet these powers are now accepted. Imagine, however, trying to persuade medieval man to believe in the technology of the future. In many respects we are like medieval man. We too are trapped in the mind-set of our time unless we make an extra effort to understand the constraints placed upon our thinking.

Western thinking is only just emerging from the straight-jacket of the scientific revolution. We have become over-dependent on scientific rationalism and we have been indoctrinated to fear the irrational and the unproven. We have divided science from religion and spirit from matter. We are newly sensing the profound strength of a holistic framework which reunites all that we have fragmented through our divisive analysis of the world. Eastern philosophy has never suffered from the mixed blessing of the scientific hand. Accordingly Eastern traditions have retained an unbroken metaphysical understanding. Both Hinduism and Buddhism have preserved esoteric teachings which incorporate a working knowledge of the chakras. In the West, such knowledge has emerged sporadically through specialised esoteric currents such as alchemy, Kabbala and Theosophy; the West has failed to secure its esoteric heritage and now comes anew to old and universal teaching.

The many world religions often appear, and indeed are, contradictory and exclusive. However, we need to remember that every religion offers both an exoteric and an esoteric. The exoteric face offers dogma and creed. It preserves and indeed upholds the outer form of religious practice. The esoteric face offers spiritual experience. Whereas the exoteric teachings are often divisive, the esoteric teachings are remarkably universal. As we approach the chakras through the ease of contemporary communication, we should not forget that this teaching derives from the esoteric tradition which is universal. The teaching that we now approach derives from the shared experiences of the awakened throughout the traditions of the world. We should follow in their footsteps with both humility and respect.

We need to understand that what we contemplate as we review the chakra blueprint is nothing less than the unfoldment of our total being, spiritual awakening. This book is no more than a beginning, yet it may point out the goal. Undertaking the tasks and responsibilities intrinsic to this personal pattern is in truth a lifetime's work. This work may be seriously undertaken under the aegis of several systems, each with its own terminology, techniques and teachers. We may profitably examine the advice presented by the Tibetan through Alice Bailey.

Awakening the Centres

The question now arises: How can this awakening and co-ordination be brought about?

The Tibetan

The Tibetan suggests the following requirements:

1 **Character building**

This may seem to be a dull and unexciting requirement. However, all spiritual movement takes place within the framework of ordinary life. This first requirement reminds us that awakening the chakras brings additional responsibilities and personal challenges. Only the rounded out personality will persevere and seriously undertake the work of shifting the focus of being to a new centre.

2 **Right motive**
The formerly closed nature of esoteric traditions was designed in part to ensure that right motive was fostered within the student – teacher relationship. The developing of right motive acts as a stabilising force against the inflation of the ego which happens all too easily.

3 **Service**
This is an active extension of right motive. Awakening the chakras brings an increased sense of connectivity to the whole, which finds its natural expression through service to others.

4 **Meditation**
This is a key inner discipline which develops sensitivities, awakens aspirations and centres the life on a spiritual note. A specialised programme of chakra meditation can only take place when meditation itself has been mastered and integrated.

5 **A technical study of the science of the centres**
The first four requirements prepare the individual in life and character to begin the next phase of personal work by absorbing the intellectual knowledge which is relevant to becoming conscious of the chakras.

6 **Breathing exercises**
The subtle energies are highly sensitive and responsive to the directed breath. Every tradition offers its own exercises in breath control. Pranayama is a complete science of itself. These techniques are best learned from an experienced spiritual teacher.

7 **Learning the technique of the will**
This seventh requirement serves to anchor the spiritual

intent generated by the first. The unfolding blueprint brings many difficult challenges which can only be surmounted by the determined.

8 **The development of the power to employ time**
This requirement once again places the onus on the student and serves to remind us that increased responsibilities require a reorganised life in which no opportunities are lost.

9 **The arousing of the Kundalini fire**
It would be wrong to introduce the chakras individually without at the same time introducing the chakras as a unity. It is a mistake to approach the seven chakras as if they were separate. The chakras are each connected one to another via the Sushumna, the subtle current within the spine. The base chakra and the crown chakra may be regarded as the two poles of magnetic force. When the intervening chakras have been sufficiently awakened and purified, the way is clear for the forces of matter and spirit to unite. The rising energies follow a curved serpentine pathway. The awakening of Kundalini, the flowering of all seven lotuses, brings mystical or cosmic consciousness.

The symbolism of the chakras

Symbolism is an instrument of knowledge and the most ancient and fundamental method of expression, one which reveals aspects of reality which escape other modes of expression.

J. C. Cooper

The chakras are traditionally represented through symbols. The functions and nature are described not through words but through symbolic images. This is the traditional approach of all esoteric traditions, for the symbol is richer in meaning than the word. Each symbol and its wide range of associations needs to be offered to the deeper levels of the mind through meditation. In fact the fullness of the symbolic code cannot be understood except through the process of meditation. The unbroken teaching lineage preserved through Laya yoga offers the age-old symbols to the contemporary world.

Each chakra is described primarily as a lotus. This flower is rooted in the mud, rises through the waters and blooms upon the surface. Here is an underlying symbolism which represents the journey from earth to spirit. Each lotus has a different number of petals which reveals the complexity of the chakra at both physical and psychic levels corresponding to the number of vortices within the chakra. These petals are also coloured in accordance with a symbolic code.

Animal symbols are attributed to the first five chakras. These express the nature of the chakra. Each of the first five chakras is also attributed to an elemental symbol. These symbols need to be integrated in meditation if we are to understand their significance. The absence of animal and elemental symbols at the sixth and seventh chakras also expresses a function of the higher centres.

The chakras, with the exception of the crown centre, are attributed a mantra, a sounded meditation which has the power to awaken the chakra through its own vibration. The mantra is accompanied by a yantra, a geometric form which again expresses the essential nature of the chakra. This too needs to be understood through the internal process of meditation. The centres are also attributed to various deities. This sacred personification reminds us of the living nature of the centres. We may approach each centre through the aegis of its presiding deity.

Let us now approach the blueprint of our being with due respect and understanding. This book only offers a beginning but let us begin in the right spirit.

Practice

- It is not difficult to become attuned to your own energy field. You might like to try the following exercise. Most people are surprised to discover that they can actually feel an emanation at the very first attempt. As with all things, practice makes perfect. The more often you do this exercise, the more success you will have.
- Sit with your palms facing but not touching one another. Slowly move the palms away from each other. Bring the palms back close together. Establish a gentle rhythm, moving together and apart in a bouncing motion. It usually happens that people quite suddenly and unexpectedly experience a feeling best described as a magnetic force. This sensation cannot be confused with general body heat or warmth. It is such a specific sensation. Close your eyes. Become aware of your breathing. On the outbreath visualise white light pouring out from the centre of the palms in a steady stream. People are both amazed and delighted when they lock onto it.
- When you experience this, you may begin to pull the hands further apart. Eventually the contact will break, and you may start again. Palm to palm contact is easiest to work with first. When you are comfortable with this you can make fingertip/fingertip contact, or use the fingertips of one hand against the palm of the other. the process of sensitising the hands to the energy field will prepare you for making contact with your own chakra energy.

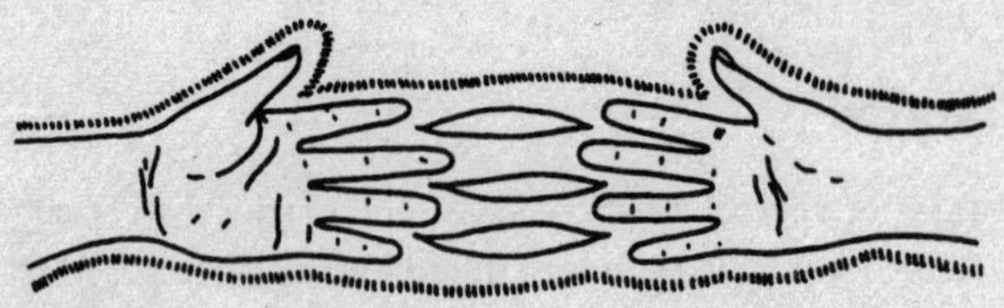

Figure 4 *Finding the etheric*

1
the first chakra

Keywords for this Chakra

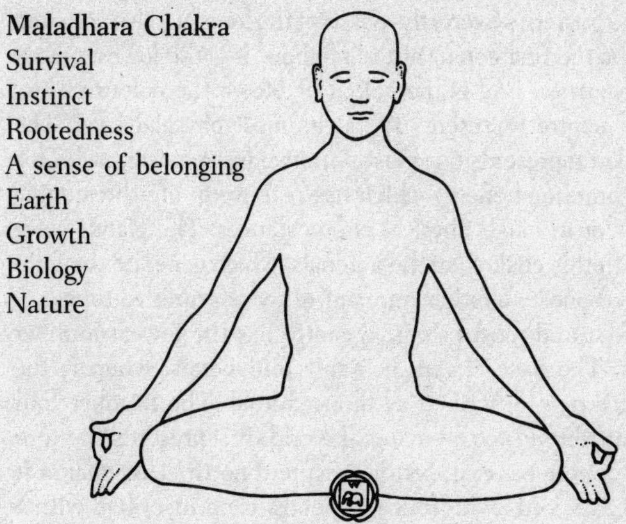

Maladhara Chakra
Survival
Instinct
Rootedness
A sense of belonging
Earth
Growth
Biology
Nature

By meditating thus on Her who shines within the Muladhara chakra, with the lustre of ten million Suns, a man becomes Lord of speech and a king among men, and an Adept in all kinds of learning.

Verse 13, Sat-Cakra-Nirupana

Establishing Roots

Our journey begins at the first chakra, which is the base chakra. It is located at the base of the spine. This first centre is called *Muladhara,* from *mula*, meaning root, and *adhara*, meaning base or support. Here we have our first clue to the function of this centre. It provides our sense of rootedness and grounding in the world. As a tree cannot stand strong without deep roots, so we cannot grow without a strong connection to the outside world through the first chakra.

In the system of Western colour attribution, the Muladhara chakra is attributed to the colour red. Coincidentally we find that in the Eastern system, the petals of the lotus are also coloured red. Red is the first colour of the rainbow. It is the lowest colour of the spectrum. Red is the colour of blood, the colour of life. This first centre represents life at its most physical level. The base chakra represents our most primitive instinct, survival. This is a raw, unrefined energy which has real use in life-threatening situations or in harsh physical circumstances. The glands associated with this chakra are the adrenals, which generate the fight or flight response, another remnant of more primitive times.

This first and most primitive centre has the fewest number of petals. The base chakra has only four petals, whereas the crown chakra is described as thousandfold. The number four is often attributed to the material world. It represents the four cardinal directions, east, south, west and north. This chakra is depicted as a lotus with four red petals, each inscribed with a letter of the Sanskrit alphabet. These letters represent the sound vibration of the nadirs connected with this centre. The element attributed to this chakra is earth, the most solid of the four elements. The mantra for this chakra is *Lam*, representing elemental earth. This mantra is sounded aloud under the supervision of a teacher when chakra awakening is consciously undertaken. It is inscribed upon the yellow background of the yellow square, Privithi, which again symbolises elemental earth. This symbol, too, is used as a focus for meditation when the active powers of this chakra are consciously sought. These specialised activities require proper tuition.

The base chakra is important as a means of establishing our contact with the physical earth. This contact is especially important to anyone seriously committed to opening the higher centres. This centre quite literally keeps us rooted. It is, however, a mistake to live as if this were the only centre. Modern gang warfare in the city streets of New York and elsewhere shows us a twentieth-century representation of life lived out through the lens of the base chakra. Here power, territory and tribal allegiance count for everything. Red blood is spilled by red-blooded men hunting for status and prestige through conquest and strength of arms. These values disappeared in the evolutionary scheme with the passing of the Stone Age. Their reappearance as life goals and values is a sad testament to contemporary city life.

Celebrating Nature

Our group attention has been turned to the earth and our relationship with it. We can no longer ignore the effects of massed human habitation. Each chakra presents us with a challenge by focusing our awareness on a particular aspect of life. It asks that we examine our relationship towards the qualities and powers expressed by the chakra. We see that eight arrows emerge from the square. These represent the many possibilities open to the individual. Curiously there are eight seasonal landmarks in the natural year. The solstice and equinox points are complemented by midway markers. These eight festivals also provide opportunities for personal growth through drawing closer to the natural rhythms of the earth.

Such festivals and celebrations were a natural and sacred part of many peoples who lived in harmony with the land. It is our loss that we have become distanced from the reality of seasonal and personal change. Our wanton destruction of nature's bounty marks the depths of our estrangement. If we wish to return to a peaceful co-operation with nature we must first acknowledge our dependency and secondly we must honour this relationship.

This chakra, the very base and foundation of physical life, begs that we question our interaction with the world around us both individually and as a group. The individual who spends all week in the office and all weekend watching television cannot be said to have a conscious relationship to the earth. On the other hand an individual who enjoys walking, gardening or simply visiting outdoor sites, might well be more aware of the changing faces of nature. However, this issue is far more than a matter of personal leisure. We need to re-examine our relationship with the natural word.

Questions

- What does living in harmony with the environment mean to you?
- Is it important for a society to celebrate its relationship with nature?
- How does contemporary Western society celebrate nature?

Harmony with The Earth

The base chakra is said to face downwards towards the ground. We are nourished by contact with the living earth and diminished through isolation from these living energies. We have an unconscious understanding of our own need to touch the earth.

We all recognise that tower blocks and concrete estates dehumanise. Green spaces, trees and gardens restore a sense of balance. The ancient Chinese art of Feng Shui, literally meaning 'wind and water', seeks to create harmony between nature and habitation, landscape and construction. The ugliness created by relying purely on functional criteria would have been quite impossible under the subtle and gentle guidelines of this art. Architects and town planners would do well to recognise that successful living must serve human need. The base chakra requires contact with natural forces. Starved of this contact the chakra will close and produce increasingly negative results.

This chakra is symbolised by Airavata, king of the elephants, who belonged to Indra, the earth god. The elephant is often also depicted with seven trunks, representing the seven minerals vital for physical life. The elephant also wears a black collar, representing the limitations of matter. Working elephants were once a common sight in India. The elephant is the largest land mammal. Its mass represents the nature of physical matter itself, heavy and gross.

In the centre of Privithi, elemental earth, we see a downward-pointing triangle. This triangle, called a trikona, represents the threefold nature of the living energies present here. Ida, Pingala and Sushumna rise from this centre. The trikona contains the linga complex, that is the phallus with its serpent coiled three-and-a-half times. This deceptively simple symbol is in effect a guide to the full gamut of powers which reside within the base chakra. We may think of the chakras as being separated one from another, yet their essential unity should never be forgotten. The seven chakras may act as a single channel when the living powers of spirit and matter fuse. This phenomenon is known as *Kundalini*. It is described as the Kundalini serpent since this power follows a winding path as it moves from centre to centre.

The intensity of such experience is almost beyond description and certainly beyond the confines of ordinary reality. If we are to comprehend the true significance and value of this sevenfold model, we need to be prepared to think deeply and abandon preconceptions. The Kundalini experience is a universal constant. It was known to the sages and wise ones of the past. It is experienced as a contemporary reality. We cannot understand the chakras without also acknowledging this unifying phenomenon. When we contemplate the dynamics of the Kundalini experience, it becomes easy to understand why this arcane branch of knowledge was for so long kept a secret to be passed on only from teacher to pupil.

The lesson of this chakra is the discovery of our personal roots. Society has become complex. Institutions which once provided a sense of continuity and belonging have gone. The need to find our roots is even more critical when family and social groups have disintegrated. Our roots lie with the earth. When we know that we are part of the living earth we have a certainty which will surpass transient social roots. Without roots, however, the individual has no sense of place and no sense of meaning. Becoming conscious of the functions of this chakra brings a sense of rootedness. Its inner state is stability. Its function is grounding.

Questions

- What is the personal and social value of a sense of belonging?
- How do you understand your own sense of rootedness?

Each chakra functions at seven levels, moving from the physical to the spiritual. Physically this chakra is related to the functions of the legs, feet, bones and large intestines. It is related to the functions of the adrenals. When this chakra is malfunctioning there is a tendency towards obesity, haemorrhoids, constipation and sciatica. At emotional levels this chakra relates to the ability to let go of past feelings. Constipation is not only physical, but emotional too. Repressed anger is definitely related to this chakra. Opening this chakra can have the effect of releasing long-held emotions.

The chakra which serves as our root support in the world is especially important as an anchor. It contains the first of the psychic knots which firmly bind spirit and matter. The move from one level of function to another can be dramatic, even within the same chakra. A barrier has to be transcended. The Brahma Granthi within the base chakra can only be transcended as we learn how to separate consciousness from matter. Active awakening enables all centres to synthesise increasingly higher energies and precipitate entry into successive levels of energy and being.

Questions

- How do you define matter?
- How do you define spirit?

It is difficult to imagine the experience of a chakra opening, but personal reports are of great value as testaments and guides for others. Hiroshi Motoyama reported the awakening of his own base chakra. He was 25 years old at the time. He had been following a daily routine of yoga and devotions for some time. After several months of continuous application he became aware of new physical sensations. He experienced an itchy feeling at the base of the spine accompanied by a tingling at the top of the head. Such experiences are not for the faint-hearted.

Motoyama reports his experiences in a matter of fact manner which belies the intensity and dynamism of the personal encounter:

> *One day when I was meditating I felt particularly feverish in the lower abdomen and saw there a round blackish-red light, like a ball of fire about to explode in the midst of white vapour. Suddenly an incredible power rushed through my spine to the top of the head and though it lasted only a second or two my body levitated off the floor.*

He remained in a feverish state for two or three days. He also felt as if his head would explode with energy. His experience was especially dramatic but not exceptional. The active awakening of this chakra may be accompanied by a temporary emotional instability.

When this chakra is open and functioning, we experience ourselves as part of nature. We have a firm sense of being rooted and of belonging. If this chakra is under-functioning, we feel isolated from the natural world and even from other people. The need to possess replaces the need to share. We experience a sense of belonging through belongings. The base chakra is undoubtedly primitive, yet that in no way implies destruction or violence – only directness and lack of pretence. To live exclusively through the base chakra is to live through the instincts. We have no need to be confined by the instinctive life. We have the power to awaken as a sevenfold being, to build upon our biological roots and become fully human.

We will draw upon a contemporary experience of greed and waste to show us our imperfect relationship with nature. The destruction of the rainforest for purely commercial gain symbolises the canker at the heart of our civilisation. This destruction represents the negative application of the powers of the Muladhara chakra. The land becomes a possession, its bounty becomes a commodity. Greed alone rules. This pattern is repeated wherever possession and ego rule.

Guided meditation – the rainforest

Imagine that you stand in a landscape newly destroyed by the loggers. The bare earth is exposed. Tree stumps stand broken everywhere, each a testimony to a tree now destroyed. The earth is battered from tyre tracks, the graze of heavy chains and the stamp of heavy boots. Leaves lie scattered over the churned earth. Piles of branches smoulder in scattered heaps. This is the field of desolation, the killing fields of nature.

You try to imagine the numbers and variety of plants that grew here but you cannot. You think about the birds and the insects, the tiny reptiles, the warm-blooded mammals, but you cannot begin to imagine their numbers. You cannot; everywhere is death. Life has been taken. You walk among the ruins dazed by the violence that still hangs in the air. This place was once home to those who lived in harmony with the world. They were driven out long ago. You hear yourself repeating 'Why?' You are filled with melancholy at this desolation, at this rape of nature. As you stand surveying the scene, you demand an answer from yourself and wonder how you might make amends for this gross invasion.

As you walk among the broken trees, you see a damaged seedling, uprooted but not destroyed. You pick it up and gently lay out its roots in the palm of your hand. You wonder about your own rootedness and relationship with the earth. You hold the seedling and resolve to give it a future. You accept a new responsibility and resolve to plant one seed in the kingdom of Earth.

Practice

- In what way may we associate the colour red with this chakra?
- What does the name *Muladhara* mean?
- What does the symbolism of the elephant teach us about this chakra?
- What does *Privithi* represent?
- Which physical systems are related to this chakra?
- What qualities might we expect when this chakra is functioning?
- Draw a circle and in it represent in some way all the activities that you associate with this chakra.

The Symbolism of the Muladhara Chakra

The lingam wrapped with 31/2 coils of the serpent shows as the home of the kundalini power. A crescent moon symbolises the divine source of all life.

The four crimson petals symbolise the four corners of the world. Each petal bears a Sanskrit letter.

The seed sound for this Chakra is *Lam*.

The yellow square Privithi represents earth.

The downward-pointing triangle shows that divine power comes from a higher level to a lower.

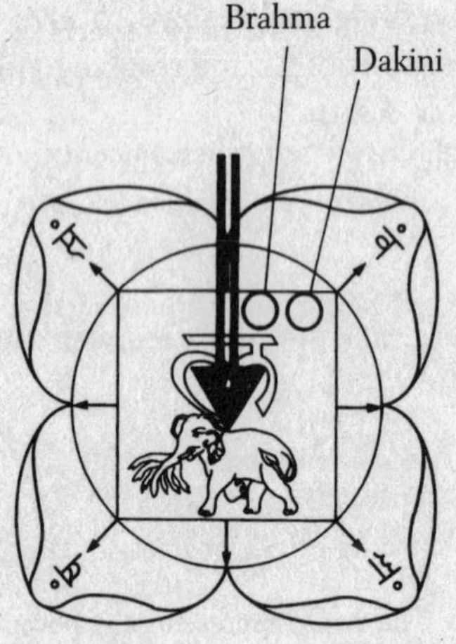

The eight arrows represent the many directions life may take.

The elephant Airavata represents the physicality of matter. The collar that he wears represents our false bondage to matter. His whiteness symbolises divinity within matter. His seven trunks represent seven qualities of human nature.

The Deities of the First Chakra

Brahma

The child Brahma has five faces which express aspects of universality, omniscience, and omnipotence. This youthful deity reminds us the consciousness of this Chakra is immature.

The **mala** is like a rosary of 108 beads. It is used with a mantra which keeps the mind focussed. *Does your spiritual intent become easily distracted?*

The **staff** symbolises the spine which is the physical channel for the life-force. Its triple prongs symbolise the three aspects of this current. *Are you ready to open to the higher levels of consciousness?*

Brahma makes a gesture which dispels fear when sincerity, intent and humility are present. *Do you have these qualities?*

The **gourd** contains a liquid which quenches spiritual thirst. *What is the nature of your spiritual thirst?*

Dakini

The goddess Dakini represents the female aspect of energy manifest.

The **sword** represents the powers of discrimination. Choosing between alternatives is a daily event. *How do you exercise choice?*

The **skull** on the staff represents the empty mind which makes space for new ideas. *Do you have space in your mind for something new?*

The **drinking cup** represents the waters of life. *What does it mean to be nourished by the living waters?*

The **spear** demands accuracy, skill and co-ordination of mind and body if the thrower is to hit the target. *What is your target in life?*

2

the second chakra

Keywords for this Chakra

Svadisthana Chakra
Intimacy
Relationships
Sharing
Sexuality
Reproduction
The unconscious

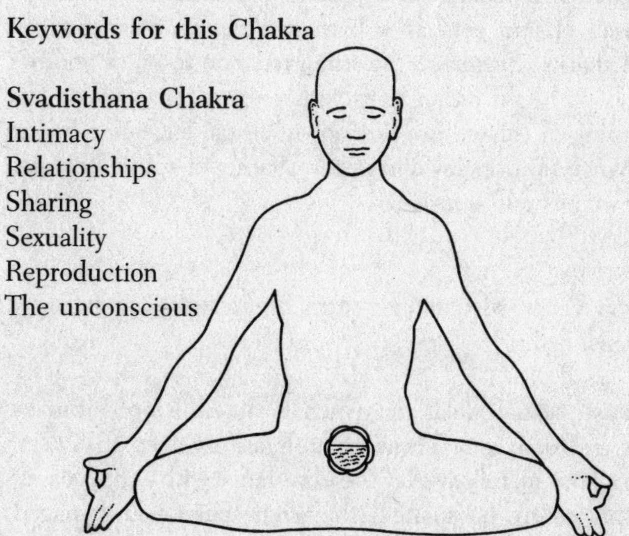

He who meditates on this stainless lotus, which is named Svadisthana, is freed immediately from all his enemies.

Verse 18, Sat-Cakra-Nirupana

Sharing Love

The second chakra is called the sacral or *Svadisthana* chakra. It is located at the coccyx in the lower abdomen adjacent to the base chakra. The sacral chakra is clearly connected with the sexual and reproductive life. Physically this chakra is related to the reproductive system, to the urinary tract, to the womb and the menstrual cycle in women and to the testes and prostatic plexus in men.

Swami Satyananda Saraswati translates *Svadisthana* as, 'one's own abode', the intimate and totally personal aspect of being. It is also translated to mean 'sweetness'. This is probably the most commonly misused chakra. When open this chakra permits deep interrelationship and connection. When this centre is closed, feelings and sexuality remain disconnected. The closed chakra acts as a barrier, a closed door to deep personal sharing. Intimacy, the true invitation to know another person, is withheld either consciously or unconsciously. The full meaning of this centre lies not in sexual exchange but in the exchange of intimacy and in the sharing of subtle energies which enriches and nourishes.

Question

- Do you easily sustain long-term friendships and intimate relationships?

By contrast, sexual violation, which is the abuse of intimacy, destroys and damages. These wounds are so deep that years do not heal but merely overlay the experience with a thin veneer. When this centre is violated, the whole person is damaged. This centre is not just the home of the physical reproductive system but is also related to the unconscious. So often, the memory of sexual violation is repressed, but its destructive effects manifest in behaviour which is unconsciously driven. We see this only too frequently in the long-term damage perpetrated by sexual abuse.

Each centre acts as a distributor of living energy to its related physical systems. When energy, for whatever reason, fails to flow fully through this chakra, physical effects are likely to appear in the related systems. Energy follows thought. In other words, unconscious fears, concealed memories or other deep patterns of disturbance have the power to freeze vitality and rob this centre of its full function. Impotence and frigidity usually have psychological components.

In the Western system of colour coding this chakra is attributed to the colour orange, a warm blend of the red from the base chakra and the yellow of the next centre. In the Eastern system, the petals of this chakra are traditionally coloured vermilion. This strong, brilliant and exciting colour symbolises ideas, impulses and desires which stimulate the mind. This chakra is related to the imagination, which is a powerful force in human creativity at all levels, spiritual, artistic and personal. The mantra for this chakra is *Vam*. The deities of this chakra are Vishnu and Sakti Rakini.

Question

- In what ways do you use your powers of imagination?

The Depths of The Unconscious

The base chakra is attributed to the element of earth, which is solid and stable. By contrast, this chakra is attributed to the element of water, which is fluid and mobile. This represents the emotional life, which is constantly changing. Rapport between people develops from a sensitivity to the moment and from an openness to each other. This chakra is represented by a mythical water creature, the Makara, a creature of the deep. We are familiar with the saying 'still waters run deep', which might be applied to this chakra with good effect. For this chakra is not only the doorway to the personal life, it is also the doorway to the unconscious mind, the true deep water.

If we are to grow as individuals we need to take the importance of the unconscious into account. We should think of the iceberg with its hidden submerged mass. The visible part may be obvious but it is nevertheless only a portion of the whole. We must take these two quite different portions into account if we are to comprehend the whole iceberg. We must take both the conscious mind and the unconscious mind into account if we are to comprehend the individual person. It is a great mistake to underestimate the influence of the unconscious mind in daily life. It follows its own hidden agenda until we give its small voice our attention.

It was Carl Jung who drew our attention to the importance of the unconscious mind for mental health and well-being. His work as a psychiatrist enabled him to understand the language of the unconscious as dream, symbol and image. Dialogue and interaction with the unconscious is vital for personal growth. The personal unconscious is like a hidden reservoir; we cannot plumb its depths yet we are reliant upon it as a source of living water. Without a free flow between these two halves of being we grow only as crippled and incomplete people. The unconscious mind stores all memories, both good and bad, positive and negative, with all the efficiency of a computer disk.

Question

- What do you consider to be the importance of the unconscious mind?

The Light of The Moon

The unconscious mind is often symbolised by the light of the moon, which is illuminated only by reflected light. In the Hawaiian Huna system, the unconscious, hidden inner self is referred to as the Lunar Self, while the conscious, rational part is referred to as the Solar Self. This division is also reflected in astrology. Health and well-being is attained when equal value is accorded to both the lunar and solar elements of being. It is therefore appropriate that we should find the Makara resting just above a crescent moon, which is the yantra for this chakra. The yantra is of course the geometric figure which expresses the energy of each centre. It can be used as a focal point for meditation. There is a curious agreement across both Eastern and Western traditions. This centre is represented on the Kabbalistic Tree of Life by the sphere of the moon.

The lunar self, the unconscious, is of great importance and should never be undervalued. There is a distinct and regrettable tendency to elevate rationality over the workings of the intuition. Indeed 'irrationality' is a word with only derogatory connotations. This schism is deep-rooted, originating with the Greeks. Working with the images and symbols of this chakra presents the opportunity to adjust this imbalance. Each chakra is given its own value as part of a whole.

Question

- Do you listen, hear and respond to your own inner voices?

Jung stressed the importance of the unconscious expression for well-being. Through his clinical practice, he recognised the presence of the unconscious in dream, spontaneous fantasy and even in simple word association. The value of these subtle activities can easily be overlooked. Yet we need to be responsive to the messages which arise from these deep waters and float gently to the surface of the mind.

The personal unconscious can be thought of as a single piece of a vast jigsaw. The combination of these many fragments forms what Jung termed the collective unconscious. This huge jigsaw, formed from the life experiences of peoples from all times and places, is imprinted by repeating key human experiences; life, death, mother, father, etc. These eternal constants are described as archetypes. The personal unconscious rests upon this greater reservoir. It is possible to access archetypal images through the higher functions of this chakra. The heightened dream life can spontaneously produce archetypal material. Indeed the archetype in its many manifestations forms the language of the collective unconscious.

These archetypal patterns take many forms and images which we instinctively recognise as being transpersonal by nature. The hero, the child, the great mother, the cosmic father, the journey, death/rebirth and adversity appear in dreams in many guises both ancient and modern. Such archetypal dreams carry an intensity and charge which makes them unforgettable; we are compelled to solve the puzzle they present for us. These rarefied psychological concepts may seem obscure and unnecessarily theoretical yet the opening of this chakra, especially if precipitated, can release a torrent of powerful images into the dream life.

Question

- Can you describe your dream life?

Far Memories

We should always remind ourselves that chakra awakening is a serious personal affair which was in the past undertaken only through a relationship with a spiritual teacher and undertaken through the safety of a traditional discipline. This is no longer the case now that the increased availability of spiritual teaching and the general rise in understanding of the group mind has empowered individuals to take responsibility for their own awakening. Nevertheless we should never underestimate the impact of disturbing the status quo. Chakra awakening has in the past been surrounded with dire warnings. The Svadisthana chakra can be especially troublesome. It houses the sexual centre, the unconscious storehouse, and to add to the potentially explosive combination, it also holds personalised karmic seeds.

Metaphysical philosophy teaches that not only are short-term single life memories related to this chakra but far memory reincarnational patterns are also found at this level of being. In other words karmic forces are related to this centre. This fact has important implications for anyone actively working with chakra energy.

The opening of this centre is usually accompanied by a generalised hypersensitivity to all stimuli. Hiroshi Motoyama describes his own experiences graphically: 'The feverish feeling I had around Svadisthana was like a mixture of ice and fire. I began to see a round crimson fire ball in my abdomen. I began to have prophetic dreams, to have ESP experiences. After awakening this chakra I became overly sensitive both physically and mentally, the smallest noise startled me.'[1] This is a very typical experience.

Expansion in the influence of this chakra is likely to bring increased activity in the dream life and a sharpened sense of unconscious needs. The opening of this chakra brings a general increase in sensitivity and specifically sharpens the kinds of senses that we normally think of as being psychic. The sixth sense is of course ever present but dormant. Greater access to the personal unconscious brings a sharpened intuition which has a wisdom of its own. Clairvoyance, direct seeing, is specifically related to this chakra. The psychic abilities are a natural part of our development as we move from a physical perception of the world to a spiritual perception through the opening of the higher centres.

Question

- What value do you place on the development of psychic faculties?

Psychism is often sought as a means in itself. However, spiritual traditions, while recognising the reality of psychic functions, stress the importance of integrated spiritual growth, not the unbalanced development of one aspect of being. Spiritual traditions affirm the wholeness of being and always stress the importance of not mistaking a staging post for the goal of the journey itself.

We will use the contemporary experience of the flotation chamber to provide an experience of this chakra.

Guided Meditation – The Flotation Chamber

Imagine that you have been invited to spend some time in a unique flotation tank. You have accepted the invitation and you are ready. You stand before its open doorway, which is like a large porthole. You remove your clothing. As you do so, realise that you are leaving behind your outer self, the persona of home and work. You step into the tank through the porthole. The water is warm and buoyant. Lie down and find that you simply float effortlessly. As you surrender to this totally pleasurable and relaxing feeling, you are reminded of the forgotten time spent in the womb. Contemplating this, you descend more deeply into your own thoughts. Here in this warm, darkened place of comfort and simplicity, you can let go of complications and confusions. This is a place of surrender to total innocence.

The soft darkness begins to warm with colour. You see that the upper surface of the chamber is transparent. A warm orange light plays over it and begins to suffuse the chamber.

Its colour reflects upon the water and floods over your body. It rises through the chamber until you lie within a total sphere of warm light.

This light will remain so long as you desire to be within it. It is attuned to you. Exercise your own control and determine for yourself how long you will remain here. The light will fade when you want it to, and you may return to the outer world, where you can put on your clothing and resume the persona of the outer life enriched by the time you have spent immersed in the waters of being.

Practice

- In what way may we relate the colour orange to this chakra?
- What does the name *Svadisthana* mean?
- What does the mythical Makara teach us about this chakra?
- What does the crescent moon symbolise?
- What physical systems are related to this chakra?
- What qualities can we expect when this chakra is functioning?
- Draw a circle and in it represent in some way all the activities that you associate with this chakra.

The Symbolism of the Svadisthana Chakra

The lotus within the lotus is called the Kunda flower.

The seed sound for this chakra is *Vam*.

The white crescent moon represents the element of water.

The six vermillion coloured petals represent the impulses, ideas and powers of the imagination, which are stimulating to the mind. Each petal bears a sanskrit letter.

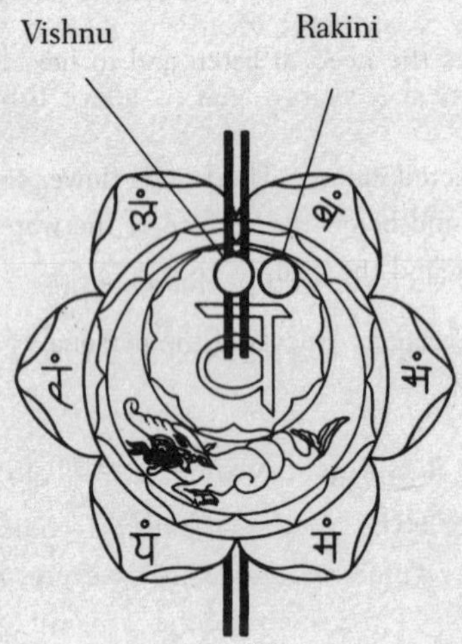

The mythical Makara, half alligator, half fish, represents the unconscious powers of the mind. The creature lies just beneath the surface. We are normally unaware of our own hidden depths. Imagination creates desires without discrimination.

The Deities of the Second Chakra

Vishnu

The god Vishnu is the second aspect of the Hindu trinity. He is Vishnu the Preserver. He wears the Vanamala, a garland made from forest flowers. It is also called the Celestial Garland.

The **disc** has to be thrown with intent and concentration if it is to hit the target. The mind, too, must be trained if it is to achieve its target.

The **conch shell** symbolises the need to listen and to hear both outwardly and inwardly.

The **lotus** symbolises the sacred journey. The Kunda flower represents the lotus both above and below the surface of the water. It symbolises both the journey and the goal.

The **mace** or war club is a weapon. Aspects of the personality and the ego have to be subdued.

Rakini

The goddess Rakini is coloured blue and has a fierce expression. This reminds the student that there is danger in the uncontrolled imagination.

The **drum** awakens the forces of this chakra.

The **trident** expresses the unity of mind, body and spirit.

The **battle-axe** symbolises the uphill battle for survival which takes place at the everyday level.

The **lotus** is a sacred flower representing the eternal journey of the soul.

3

the third chakra

Keywords for this Chakra

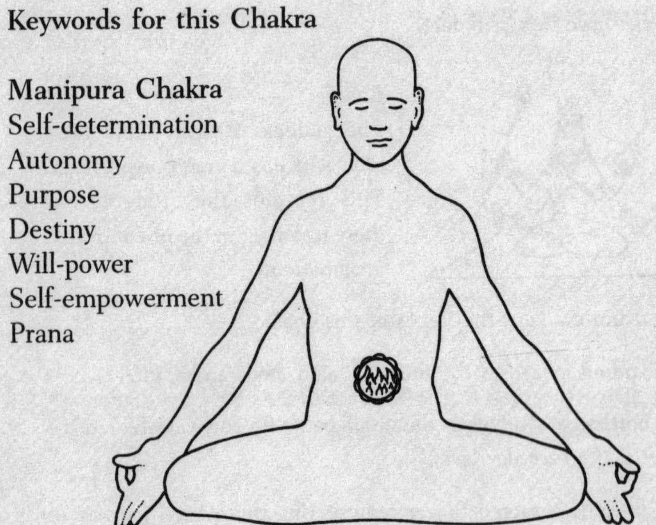

Manipura Chakra
Self-determination
Autonomy
Purpose
Destiny
Will-power
Self-empowerment
Prana

Meditate there on the regions of Fire, triangular in form and shining like the rising sun.

Verse 20, Sat-Cakra-Nirupana

The Inner Sun

As we move upwards on our journey through the chakras, we now reach the third chakra. We have moved from the centre symbolising elemental earth to the centre symbolising elemental water. We now encounter elemental fire. We have moved from the functions of survival and reproduction to the centre representing the sense of self and place in the world. We have moved from the relative simplicity of the fourfold lotus to the growing complexity of the sixfold lotus. Now we reach the tenfold lotus. This chakra is depicted with ten petals coloured a smoky purple. We have arrived at the third chakra.

According to the Western system, this chakra is attributed to the colour yellow. We naturally relate positively to this bright, strong colour. It is of course the colour of the sun which is at the centre of our solar system. The solar plexus chakra is often likened to the personal sun. It is the personal furnace, the storehouse of life energies. The element of fire is attributed to this chakra. Its animal symbol is the red ram which is sacred to the fire god Agni. Its yantra is the embellished downward-pointing triangle which symbolises dynamic spiritual activity.

This centre is called *Manipura*, which can be translated as 'filled with jewels' or 'city of jewels'. The mantra *Om Mane Padme Hum*, translates as Hail to the Jewel in the Lotus. Gemstones were often forged from the fires of the inner earth. This centre is related to the process of transformation symbolised by the action of fire.

Question

- What do you understand by the term transformation?

The Manipura chakra is located at the solar plexus, the abdomen. It is rooted between the twelfth thoracic vertebra and first lumbar vertebra. It governs the digestive system, the liver, spleen, stomach and small intestines. It is related to the functions of the pancreas gland. When malfunctioning, physical disorders such as ulcers, diabetes and eating disorders can arise. The malfunctioning of this chakra also manifests in distortions of will-power, as the wilful and self-obsessed, or as the timid person who is too easily directed by others or by circumstances. Physically this centre turns food into fuel by extracting energy from raw material. This is a centre of transformation both physical and emotional.

The digestive function of this centre serves to focus our attention on the quality of food that we eat. In the age of convenience food, we should not allow ourselves to be led totally astray from the notion of living food. Living food bears *prana*, the universal life-force. The Manipura chakra is an important storehouse and distributor of prana throughout the body. Prana is said to divide into five types, called winds. Each type of prana governs a different area of the body. *Apana* operates from the navel to the base of the anus. *Samana* operates through the upper abdomen. *Prana vayu* operates through the chest region. *Usana vayu* operates through the head and limbs. *Uyanu vayu* operates through the entire body. Knowledge of these subtle forces is called *Prana Vidya*, the knowledge of prana. This is a complete esoteric science which raises consciousness through a growing awareness of prana and its conscious direction. Each chakra is a centre of prana but the Manipura chakra is its storehouse in the body. This centre can be awakened by drawing up apana, the prana which flows below the navel while at the same time drawing down prana vayu, which flows from the navel to the throat. The simultaneous collision of these two powers generates a powerful energy in the Manipura centre. Such exercises and techniques can only be passed on by experienced teachers to serious and committed students.

Prana is a subtle energy. It can be directed through the body by the concentrated use of the mind. It is highly responsive to the controlled breath allied to the directed thought. This is the basis of the science of *pranayama*. Pranayama can only be taught under the guidance of an experienced teacher within the framework of an established group. Nevertheless we may appreciate its key principle, which is the awakened awareness of prana. Prana is important for health, well-being and for the unfolding of the higher senses. Prana exists naturally in clean air, fresh flowing waters, unspoilt landscape and living food. Its quality is destroyed as we pollute the air, the waters, the landscape and even our food. It is a curious fact that a small number of sainted beings throughout history have lived almost without food. Such people have lived upon pure spiritual energy – that is, on prana. The ordinary person in the street still requires good, pure food. Nevertheless this rare phenomenon points us towards the untapped powers of this chakra.

Encountering Fire

One of the most extraordinary and almost forgotten powers of this chakra is *Tumo*, the generation of psychic heat. This phenomenon was refined in the cold lands of Tibet. This specialised training culminated in a punishing test as the candidates were wrapped in wet sheets dipped in the icy waters. Each candidate had to dry as many sheets as possible by the generation of psychic heat. The test continued from dusk until daybreak, when the winning candidate was declared. Such feats are clearly far more than idle fancy. We should remind ourselves that the Manipura is the centre of elemental fire, its animal symbol is the ram which is sacred to the god of fire, Agni. The great teacher Milarepa mastered this practice under the direction of his teacher Marpa. Milarepa survived an entire winter in a freezing cave using the concentrated visualisations, breath control and directed thought of the tumo practice. He even wrote a long poem about his unexpected trial.

During that time of calamity,
The snow, the wintry blast and my thin cotton garment fought against each other on the white mountain.
The snow as it fell on me, melted into a stream,
The roaring blast was broken against the thin cotton robe which enclosed fiery warmth,
The life and death struggle of the fighter could there be seen
And I, having won the victory, left a landmark for the hermits
Demonstrating the great virtue of tumo.

from *Magic and Mystery in Tibet,* by Alexandra David-Neel

Prana is a subtle yet tremendously powerful energy, as tumo shows us. It can be directed internally through the body or externally to another person. A great deal of healing takes place through the interchange of subtle energy. The abilities related to this chakra are telepathy, clairvoyance, clairaudience and the ability to send prana. Motoyama reported the awakening of this chakra:

I often saw another reddish light centred on the navel that would become intensely white, seemingly much brighter than the sun. I began to see a purple light shining between my eyebrows. I was endowed with such enhanced ESP as clairvoyance, telepathy and spiritual insight. Emotionally the result of awakening the Manipura chakra was that my emotions somehow became richer and more under my control. I also acquired a much deeper level of sympathy with people.[1]

This centre is clearly related to the emotional life. The stomach is, after all, highly sensitive to our emotional states. We feel panic, fear, shock and anxiety through the stomach. We feel numb, we feel sick, we feel a knot in the stomach. Our emotions are registered through the body but especially through the solar plexus. The full range of human emotions from grief to joy, from sorrow to elation, should be experienced, not denied; this is the very stuff of the human condition. Nevertheless the symbolism of this chakra reminds us that powerful emotions have the power to become all-consuming. The purple-coloured petals which in the Eastern tradition serve to represent the diminished light of an oppressive rain cloud, remind us that our perspective on life can become clouded when we take too personal an outlook. Rudra as an aspect of Vishnu also symbolises the emotional life. He proffers the mala or rosary to the student as a reminder that emotions also have divine expression through devotion.

Question

- How do you respond to emotions?

The will to be

This centre is intimately related to the personal will, which may be thought of as the personal fire. We easily think of will in terms of the driving fire of ambition, self-mastery and self-determination. The will is a powerful force for good or ill. It can be used to achieve a long-term goal, to overcome a serious obstacle, or to thwart – even subvert – the will of others. This personal fire feeds the will, the drive to make a personal statement and to express an inner drive. Will is an elusive yet clearly powerful human quality. We see it clearly in circumstances of extraordinary hardship and suffering when the individual refuses to be broken by the power exercised by another. The solar plexus is our place of empowerment. Self-expression and the rightful use of will as self-determination are of great personal importance.

Questions

- How do you define the personal will?

- What in your opinion is the proper use of personal will?
- What in your opinion is the improper use of personal will?
- Do you have a sense of your direction in life, in the short term and in the long term?

The contemporary phenomenon of the eating disorder seems to express a deep personal rebellion when significant others, parents, partners or authority figures have rendered the individual helpless to make personal decisions. The body becomes the battleground where conflicts of power are waged. It is perhaps no surprise that this centre should take on this new function as final bastion of the will. Eating disorders, whether anorexia or bulimia, are now understood as being defiant expressions of will, extreme acts of self-assertion where other more usual avenues for self-empowerment appear blocked. With the increase in stress and the decrease in avenues for self-expressive release of unconscious tension, the perfectly ordinary eating function has become a vehicle for issues of personal will.

This centre represents an important staging post on the path of becoming. Utilising power and responsibility under will are difficult challenges. The awakened power of this centre brings a rightful sense of self which leads naturally to a continuously expanding view of self. Too often the journey ceases at this point. It is possible to function in contemporary society by drawing only upon a modicum of energy from the first three chakras. The will to survive, the will to reproduce, and the will to be are the basic essentials for modern life. Indeed the Tibetan has pointed out that most live below the diaphragm. Those who have begun consciously to draw upon the sevenfold blueprint in all its depth and complexity richness and splendour will, however, never be content with a shallow and incomplete existence when transformation remains a possibility.

We may actively use the transformative powers of this centre. Spend time in preparation, reflecting on your own use of will in the world. Decide how you wish to change and improve your response. Perhaps you have a hasty temper, an inability to listen to another's point of view, perhaps you cannot bear not getting your own way; the will has many subtle nuances. Write down all the things that you wish to leave behind. When you feel thoroughly prepared, undertake the following visualisation.

Guided Meditation – The Flame of Transformation

Find yourself standing before a pair of double doors which seem very ancient. Beside the doors hangs a bell-rope. You pull the rope and immediately a loud, clear note fills the air. The doors swing open. You enter the room. You find that you stand in a dimly lit domed chamber. The curved ceiling is transparent yet only a little light enters at present. On the floor, set in mosaics, you see the pattern of the Manipura chakra with its ten petals. You see the image of the ram in a brilliant red tile.

You remember that this is the place of elemental fire and you know that fire consumes, purges and purifies. In the centre of the chakra image stands a tripod with a dish of hot coals burning bright red. Step forward holding your paper. This represents your true inner will. You have already expressed your willingness to seek out your true will. Stabilise your intent and when you are ready place your list in the flame. See these old patterns being consumed. Watch until the flame has disappeared. Suddenly light fills the chamber from above. Glorious yellow sunlight enters the chamber; everything is clear and bright by this new light.

When the flames die down, look closely into the ashes and there you will see the tiny glint of a golden drop. If you have the courage, take it from the dying embers, for it is yours by right.

Practice

- In what way may we relate the colour yellow to this chakra?
- What does the name *Manipura* mean?
- What does the symbolism of the ram tell us about this chakra?
- What does the downward-pointing triangle teach us about this chakra?
- Which physical systems are governed by this chakra?
- What qualities might we expect when this chakra is functioning?
- Draw a circle and in it represent in some way all the activities that you associated with this chakra.

The Symbolism of the Manipura Chakra

The seed sound for this chakra is *Ram*.

The ram is sacred to the fire god, Agru. It represents powerful emotions which cloud insight.

The downward-pointing triangle represents the continuous downflow of spiritual presence. The triangle is coloured red to symbolise spiritual fire.

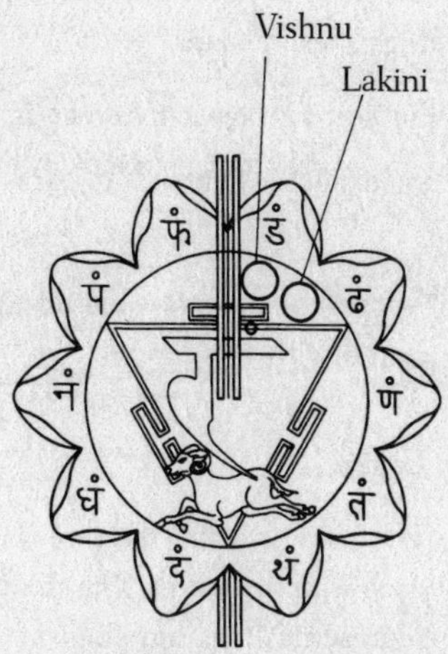

The 10 petals, the colour of a heavy raincloud, symbolise a veil which clouds our inner vision. This has to be burned away, through the effort of personal transformation.

The Deities of the Third Chakra

Vishnu

Vishnu, the Preserver, appears in the guise of Rudra, who symbolises the powerful emotions.

The **mala**, like a rosary, symbolises the need to transform emotions into higher expressions.

The **fire weapon** symbolises the searing power inherent in the emotions. It stresses the need to express the emotions without being consumed by them.

The **abhayamudra** gesture dispels fear.

The **varada** gesture grants boons.

Lakini

The goddess Lakini has three faces, each with three eyes. The third eye represents the opening of the psychic senses.

The **Vajra** symbolises the thunderbolt which brings enlightenment suddenly and with great force.

The **fire weapon** symbolises the fiery nature of this chakra, which has the power to either destroy or transform.

The **varada** gesture grants boons.

The **abhayamudra** gesture dispels fear.

4

the fourth chakra

Keywords for this Chakra

Anahata Chakra
Transpersonal love
Universal compassion
Unconditional love
Limitless
Infinite

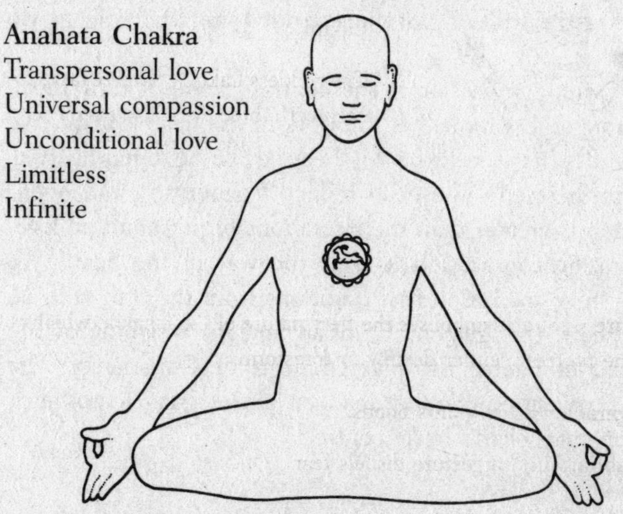

This lotus, is like the celestial wishing tree.

Verse 26, Sat-Cakra-Nirupana

Unconditional Love

We now reach the place of the heart chakra, yet we have crossed an abyss in consciousness which is only too rarely experienced. The first three chakras represent the most basic human needs; we are now moving onto levels which represent not a need but a blessing, not self-satisfaction but generous, selfless outpouring.

The heart is a familiar symbol. Yet this chakra is not associated with the personal love for the sweetheart nor with the sorrow of the broken heart. The heart chakra is also called the Abode of Mercy. This is the centre for a universalised love which is not limited to loved ones and those who love us in return. It is the compassion for the stranger; it is the loving kindness for the greater human family. This love is purely altruistic. There can be nothing to gain except the gift of giving itself. Personal love is often manipulative, impersonal love is transcendent and seeks nothing in return. Never have we been so aware of the suffering of the extended human family as we are today.

Generating compassion is the central theme of Buddhism. Exchanging others for self is the work of the heart chakra. We understand what it is to be 'big-hearted', to be 'open-hearted' and 'warm-hearted'. These all reflect a generosity and openness which is greater than the limitations of personalised love.

Generating compassion is truly the way of the heart. We find this in so many spiritual traditions from the Sufi with its winged heart, the Ancient Egyptian and its Weighing of the Heart and of course the pierced heart of Christianity. The Tibetan, a twentieth-century teacher, places great importance on the opening of the heart centre:

The first centre which the aspirant seeks consciously to energise and on which he concentrates during the early stages of his noviciate, is the heart centre. He has to learn to be group conscious, to be sensitive to group ideals, and to be inclusive in his plans and concepts; he has to learn to love collectively and purely, and not be actuated by personality attraction, and the motive of reward. Until there is this awakening he cannot be trusted to wield the powers of the throat centre, for they would be subordinated to self aggrandisement and ambition of various kinds.[1]

The Way of The Heart

The way of feeling is much devalued in the West. It is distrusted for its subjectivity and despised for its irrational basis. Instead we have elevated the rational mind into a false god. The intellect is dangerously overvalued. Spiritual traditions have always accorded a value to the rational mind as a tool, not a goal. Ironically enough, science itself, the supreme testament to the logical and the analytical, may begin to dent our faith in the power of rationality. We have identified thinking as the key factor in the evolution of consciousness, but this may prove not to be the case. Scientific debate is giving rise to a radical new view which sees consciousness and emotions as deeply interwined and inseparable. Feelings, of course, whether physically based, like hunger and pain, or emotional, directly touch us. We cannot ignore their immediate impact. Thoughts, abstracted experience, lack this directness. Traditionally the head has been associated with thinking while the heart has been associated with feeling. There can be little doubt that we come from a culture dominated by the head: its effects are plain to see. None the less, feelings may yet prove to be an important key in the evolution of consciousness.

Questions

- How do you respond to life, from the head or the heart?
- What is the value of transpersonal love?

The Western mind is so paralysed by science that we are unable to make any leap of faith without a scientific justification. We have now taken up meditation with enthusiasm, encouraged by science's announcement that meditation affects brain patterns. The final irony will come when science informs us that we should abandon our quest for the rational and take up our feelings with intensity and passion. Science will reinstate the way of the heart, the path of compassion and wisdom.

We in the West are very uncomfortable with the intangible and the unseen, aptly represented by elemental air which is attributed to this chakra. As we have moved through the chakras, we have moved from the solid and the tangible towards the abstract. Air is of course invisible yet omnipresent. It is vital for life and shared by all. It is a perfect symbol for the quality of compassionate love which it represents. To reinforce the attribution of air, we find the gazelle, sacred to the goddess Kakini. This graceful creature bounds through the air as it moves.

In the Western system of correspondences, this chakra is traditionally attributed to the colour green, the colour of new growth and new life. It is of course the colour we naturally associate with the first blush of spring. The Egyptians observed the same thing as the new season's papyrus burst into life. Green was, for the Egyptians too, the colour of rebirth. Green is an appropriate colour for the birth of a new level of feeling within ourselves.

The deities of this chakra are Isa, as lord of speech, an aspect of Shiva, and Kakini. Though we normally associate the powers of communication with the throat chakra, the heart chakra has its own speech, namely poetry, the speech of the heart. Poetry of course is a wonderfully defiant art which cannot be reduced to rationality. It expresses meaning through the non-rational. Gopi Krishna experienced the full opening of all the chakras over a number of years. In his autobiography he records how he spontaneously began to write in poetry. To his own great astonishment he also began to write in languages which were unknown to him. He wrote in Persian, German, French, Italian, Arabic as well as the familiar Kasmiru and Sanskrit: 'The lines developed in an extremely subtle form, an invisible seed and instantaneously passed before my mind as fully formed verses following each other in rapid succession until the whole page was completed.'[2]

The name of this chakra, *Anahata*, means 'unstruck'. It refers to a subtle ability to hear a sound which is made but not struck in the same way that a gifted poet receives poetic inspiration. Only the sensitive may hear the subtle sound.

Motoyama's experiments also revealed an important difference between the first three centres and the succeeding group beginning at the heart chakra. The first three chakras are characterised by psychic powers which are by nature receptive. These include telepathy, ESP, psychometry and clairvoyance. However, the awakened heart chakra brings powers which are literally outgoing and generative. It is traditionally said that the awakened heart chakra brings the ability to actualise desires in the outside world. Motoyama found that the opened Anahata chakra brought psi-powers, psychokinesis and psychic healing which had the power to affect the external world.

This chakra contains what is described as the Vishnu Granthi, which is a knot of energy. Similar knots are located in the base chakra, the Muladhara, and in the brow chakra, the Ajna. These knots can only be loosened by cumulative work within the individual psyche. These barriers represent particularly important landmarks on the journey. Each represents a passage through and beyond certain mind-sets which normally inhibit and limit. The loosening of the Vishnu Granthi represents the transition from the small-self to the greater self.

The Wish-fulfilling Tree

This chakra has a subsidiary chakra which is regarded as the inner court of the Anahata chakra itself. It is symbolised by a red lotus of eight petals. It contains an island of gems which holds an altar and a tree, the *Kalpa* or wishing tree. Though present in all, this subsidiary chakra only functions when the Anahata has been awakened. Here the student offers devotion to the guru or teacher. The secondary chakra is described in the sacred literature in the following way:

Let him find in his heart a broad ocean of nectar,
within it a beautiful island of gems,
Where the sands are bright golden and sprinkled with jewels.
Fair trees line its shores with a myriad of blooms,
And within it rare bushes, trees, creepers, and rushes,
On all sides shed fragrance most sweet to the senses.

Who would taste the sweetness of divine completeness
Should picture therein a most wonderful tree,
On whose far-spreading branches grow fruit of all fancies –
The four mighty teachings that hold up the world.
There the fruit and the flowers know no death and no sorrows,
While to them the bees hum and soft cuckoos sing.
Now, under the shadow of that peaceful arbour
A temple of rubies most radiant is seen.
And he who shall seek there will find on that seat rare,
His dearly Beloved enshrined therein.
Let him dwell with his mind, as his teacher defines
On that Divine Form with its modes and signs

from *Yoga*, translated by Ernest Wood

It is said that when the Anahata chakra is opened, wishes are spontaneously fulfilled through the activity of the Kalpa tree. Yet this wish-fulfilling centre may only open when the desire for the fulfilment of all personal wishes has been totally transcended. The full powers of this chakra indicate that personal karma has been completely absorbed, for this chakra is not subordinate to karmic forces.

The modern sage Sai Baba provides an astonishing example of this. He heals and is said to appear in more than one place simultaneously. Numerous testaments recount that he spontaneously manifests gifts, the very heart's desire for those who seek him out. Sai Baba says, 'I shall tell you why I give these rings, talismans, rosaries, etc. It is to mark the bond between me and those to whom they are given.'[3] However, though Sai Baba is able to fulfil wishes for others, he creates nothing for himself; his heart's desire is to fulfil the heart's desire of others. We see here the mark of one who has truly awakened this centre. Imagine for a moment that you are given the power to manifest all hearts' desires. How would you use this gift? If your first thought is for yourself, then you still need to journey.

Question

- If the gift of fulfilling wishes was granted to you, how would you use it?

Critics of Sai Baba simply refuse to accept that the laws of nature as generally understood can be transcended with such consummate ease. Questioning the very foundations of belief, especially scientific belief, is of course profoundly disturbing, yet Sai Baba is not alone. The English healer Geoff Boltwood who has none of the fame nor following of Sai Baba also shares some of the same gifts. He too materialises perfumed healing oil and crystals. Sounds manifest in his presence. Such sounds are 'unstruck' appearing from no visible source. Like Sai Baba, he says that the gifts he manifests are not party tricks but a sign that they are receiving a spiritual gift and that their perceptions can change.[4]

Question

- Who represents cosmic love for you?

According to tradition, the opening of this centre awakens transpersonal love, it brings an increased ability to direct prana, especially for healing. It permits a detached comprehension of karmic influences and generates poetic wisdom. Wishes are spontaneously granted, cosmic love is awakened. We may see the qualities and powers at work in the world if we look hard enough.

Hiroshi Motoyama recorded the awakening of the heart chakra in the following way:

> *One morning the following occurred. I saw a kind of heat energy rising from my coccyx to my heart through my spine. My chest felt very hot and I saw my heart start to shine a brilliant gold. As the kundalini rose from my heart to the top of my head it became shining white. Since then I have been able to do psychic healing. I learned to control the abilities to emit psi energy. My psychological state also underwent some profound changes with the awakening, I developed an attitude of non-attachment to worldly things.*

This is the true meaning of the heart, not the sentimental love of star-struck lovers but the glimpse of a cosmic love which binds all.

The fairy tale of the Snow Queen presents a wonderful metaphor for the heart frozen by false and mistaken love. In the end, true love, symbolised by Gerda's quest, is triumphant. Her love, the love of the heart, frees Kay from his imprisonment. We will use these archetypal images too, for we will speak to the inner heart.

Guided Meditation – The Rose of the Heart

Find yourself alone in a great hall cut entirely from ice. It has a cold beauty. The floor and walls give off a strange blue light which gives every angle and line a sharp edge. Though it must be cold here, you do not feel it. In places the walls are so thin that you can see beyond. Through the translucent ice you make out shambling, huddling figures. Frozen by icy blasts, they attempt to bury themselves in their thin shawls. A mother holds her child close. You see their pale faces but you are uninterested in their plight and return to your inner world of cold beauty.

Great mirrors are set in the walls of ice. You parade before them admiring yourself. Somewhere from your memory banks something stirs. Images of a time outside the ice palace begin to flicker. You see yourself as a newborn baby, helpless and dependent on the love of another. You recall the feel of human warmth and the inner warmth of another's joy. Images begin to appear in the mirror, called up by your own memories. A face, kindly and gentle begins to form as you watch. You have known human love at least once, perhaps even briefly. Allow these memories and feelings to develop. As they grow, more pictures fill the mirror of your mind. You see the face of one who has loved you in the mirror. The image is so strong now that you reach out to touch them. As you do so, they step out from the mirror. This person, who first showed you love, will now render you another great service. They reach out towards your heart and extract a silver of ice as sharp as a blade. You hear the words:

The coldness of the intellect is misplaced here.

The sharpness of the mind is dangerous here.

The pride of the rational is false here.

A hand is placed over the wounded heart and warmth floods your body. In that same moment you hear the sound of cracking ice. Everything about you is disintegrating, the walls of ice tumble. As the great blocks fall, they simply disappear. For they were held up only by your thoughts. The image of your loving friend is fading too. Yet there is time to offer your thanks. Finally you stand alone, in your hand a tiny but perfect rosebud. From the distance you hear the cry of a child. You set out on a new journey.

Practice

- In what way may we relate the colour green to this chakra?
- What does the name *Anahata* mean?
- What does the symbolism of the gazelle tell us about this chakra?
- What does the symbol of the interlaced triangles teach us about this chakra?
- Which physical systems are governed by this chakra?
- What qualities might we expect if this chakra is functioning?
- Draw a circle and in it represent in some way all the activities that you associate with this chakra.

The Symbolism of the Anahata Chakra

The seed sound for this chakra is *Yam*.

The gazelle, sacred to the Kakini, bounds through the air. We too may briefly experience moments of spiritual liberation before we touch earth again.

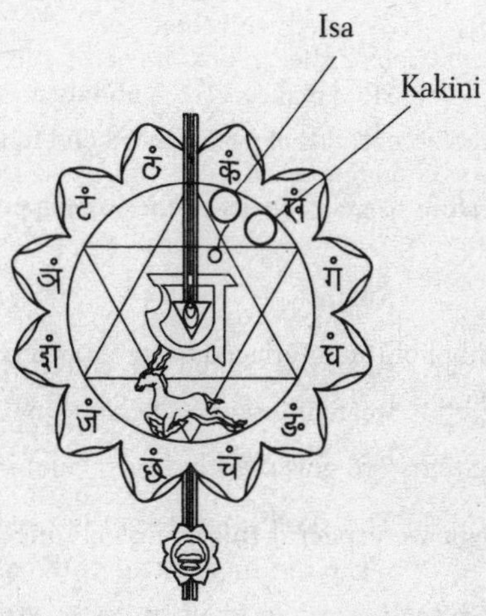

The two interlaced triangles represent the place where the divine and the human may meet in balance. A droplet of divine nectar falls from the crescent moon within the interior triangle.

The Kalpa or Kalpaturu is called the Celestial Wishing Tree. It is found in a subsidiary chakra of eight petals.

The Deities of the Fourth Chakra

Isa

Isa is the Lord of Speech. He is depicted with a black antelope. He is another form of Shiva. He is depicted with three eyes.

He makes the **abhayamudra** gesture to dispel fear in the three worlds of past, present and future.

He makes the **varada** gesture to grant boons to the worshipper.

Kakini

Kakini is yellow in colour. She wears the skin of the antelope and has three eyes.

The **skull** symbolises the need to retain the empty mind. If the mind is full of theories and explanations there is no space for experience.

The **noose** symbolises the fact that we must be wary of being trapped by our own spiritual experiences. These are events upon the journey not goals in themselves.

The **abhayamudra** gesture dispels fear.

The **varada** gesture grants boons.

5

the fifth chakra

Keywords for this Chakra

Vishuddi Chakra
Creativity
Communication
Self-expression
Direct talking
Sound
Vibration

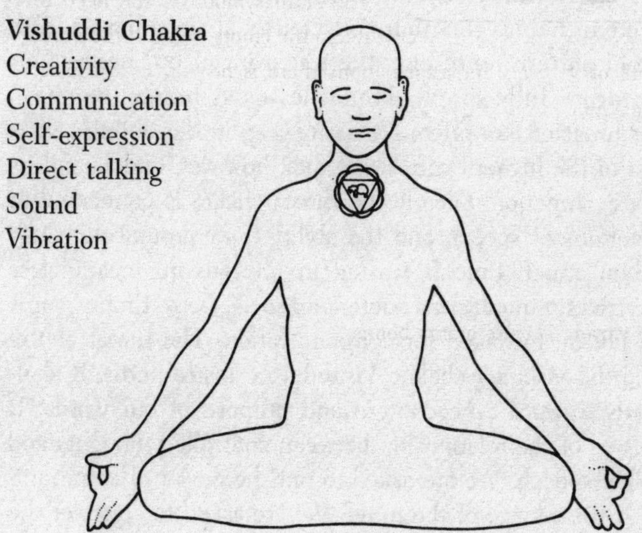

This region is the gateway of the great Liberation for him who desires the wealth of Yoga and whose senses are pure and controlled.

Verse 30, Sat-Cakra-Nirupana

Purification

As we rise through the chakras we need to remind ourselves that the higher states of consciousness are less frequently encountered in ordinary life. We may therefore find it difficult to recognise these qualities both in ourselves and others. It is possible to function in life through the first three centres which establish survival, reproduction and will-power. True compassion is a rare quality. The rarefied qualities of the final three centres are even less frequently encountered. However, general interest in metaphysical areas and a real commitment to personal growth is contributing to generalised raising of consciousness. Rather than perceive higher states as being outside the norm, we should anticipate the time when ordinary human beings function consciously at these levels. The sevenfold pattern represents the blueprint of our being. Our failure to live fully simply diminishes us as human beings.

The throat chakra offers a massive leap in our abilities. It is the first of the higher centres. We may, however, understand its most basic function. Clearly the throat chakra is connected to the functions of speech and the ability to communicate. Only think how much time is wasted in idle gossip, meaningless chatter, pseudo-intellectual banter and social froth. Empty words should not be mistaken for communication. The throat centre is called the *Vishuddi* chakra. Vishuddi means to purify. It challenges us to purify the content and purpose of our words. It reminds us of the relationship between controlled thoughts and controlled speech. We are asked to put the power of communication at the service of the mind. We are asked to consider the power of words. In our media-ridden culture we are only too aware of the destructive force of words. Let us instead contemplate how words may be used to unite, to heal and to reconcile.

Questions

- How do you use words?
- Do you always say what you mean and mean what you say?

Allied with the function of speech and communication, we find that this chakra represents the quality of hearing. This appears to be a very ordinary quality. However, even in its mundane application we should question how well we truly hear what others are saying. The cry for help is rarely verbal, yet it is as long and loud as any scream. We are selectively deaf when it suits us. If the outer ear is closed, how can the inner ear be opened? The words of others are easily heard; the guiding words of the inner voice can only be heard when the chatter of the mind has been stilled. When the mind is full of noise, there can be no room for the still, small voice. It is the practice of meditation which gradually quietens the mind and provides a space in which the inner voice can be heard.

Hiroshi Motoyama experienced this personally: 'Since the vishuddi awakened I have been able to hear much more clearly, not with my physical ear but with that of the mind.'[1] The opening of the inner ear can only take place when the individual becomes spiritually polarised. The quality of inner hearing is a development of the refined sensitivity which was awakened in the heart centre. The ability to hear the 'unstruck' sound is extended even further. The normal range of hearing extends between 20 and 30 hertz. We in fact listen in at a very small window of the universe. Our mistake lies in confusing this small frame with totality. If our hearing were to extend beyond these parameters, our perception of reality would be dramatically expanded.

Question

- Are you aware of an inner voice?

The Mysteries of Sound

This chakra is intimately connected with the power of sound. We now live in a sea of indiscriminate sound from the radio, the television and even the portable sound box. We simply take sound for granted. We utilise sound almost exclusively for its entertainment value, we have lost sight of other more ancient dimensions of sound to change consciousness and even to heal. Sounded meditation, mantra, is a complete branch of meditation practice in itself. Each chakra has its own seed sound, the sound which resonates to the natural vibration of each centre. The mantra for this chakra is *Ham*. The most famous mantra remains *Aum*. The Tibetan speaks of the purifying effects of this sound: 'So let the Aum do its work and let all of you who can employ it with frequency and with right thought so that the world purification may proceed a pace.'[2]

A sound is vibration; vibration creates form. Hans Jenny demonstrated this with great clarity when he showed that waveforms acting on liquids and powders produced geometric patterns. He built a tonoscope which rendered sound uttered into a microphone into their visual representation. He discovered that the sounded mantra Om actually produced its own yantra, the now famous geometric shape of diminishing triangles within a circular form (see Figure 5.1).

Figure 5.1 Sound as pattern

Sacred traditions, whether Eastern or Western, have always retained their link with the sacred sound through both chant and music. We should not ignore the principles which underlie these traditions. Our profoundly secular world is much impoverished by the loss of the sacred in all the arts. A revival in the restorative powers of music and sound has reaffirmed its importance for our well-being. The erratic heartbeat of the premature baby calms to the sound of the mother's singing. The St Patrick's Hospital in Montana includes a full repertoire of music both sung and played for the sick, the comatose and the dying.

Good Vibrations

Ever since the 1960s there has been much loose talk about raising vibrations. Over-used though this phrase may be, it should not be dismissed. For the past twenty years, Valerie Hunt, a professor of kinesiology, has measured human electromagnetic output under different conditions. Using an electro-myograph, which records the electrical activity of the muscles, Hunt, like Motoyama, recorded radiations emanating from the body at the sites traditionally associated with the chakras. Through her research she made the startling discovery that certain types of consciousness were related to certain frequencies.

She found that when the focus of a person's consciousness was anchored in the physical world, their energy field registered the frequencies in the range of 250 cps (cycles per second). This is close to the body's own biological frequency. Active psychics and healers, however, registered in a band between 400 and 800 cps. Trance specialists and chanellers registered in a narrow field of 800–900 cps, but from 900 cps onwards Hunt correlated what she termed 'mystical personalities' who had a firm sense of the cosmic interconnections between everything. They were anchored in reality, possessed psychic and healing abilities, were able to enter deep trance states, yet had transcended and unified the separate experiences through a mystic, holistic, metaphysical philosophy.

Question

- Where is your consciousness focused?

We may place these findings alongside our journey through the chakras. As we move up through the centres, each represents a higher vibration which brings its own particular qualities and powers. The awakened throat chakra is far removed from the base chakra in terms of both vibration and function. The base chakra represents survival, the throat chakra communication; the base chakra represents the primitive sense of smell, the throat chakra the refined sense of inner hearing. The base chakra represents earth, the throat chakra spirit, *akasa*. The first four chakras move through the elements of earth, water, fire and air. This fifth element symbolises the mystery that is life itself. Akasa is represented by the Akasamandala, the circle within the downward-pointing triangle. This represents a gateway into transcendent levels. In the Western system this chakra is attributed to blue, the colour of the sky. Like *akasa*, the sky symbolises that which is ever-present, omnipresent and beyond our grasp. The limitless expanse of the sky reminds us that this chakra symbolises a consciousness free from matter. By analogy, flying dreams are usually accompanied by a great sense of freedom and delight. The return to the waking state is an unwelcome intrusion. Few travellers have experienced such exalted realms. Even fewer record their experiences. Gopi Krishna, however, was a faithful if sometimes unwilling traveller. He was frequently plunged into cosmic states without warning. We who can only wonder at such unusual states of consciousness can only hear his words and imagine:

> *I had expanded in an indescribable manner into a titanic personality, conscious from within of an immediate and direct contact*

> *with an intensely conscious universe, a wonderful inexpressible immanence all about me. The shoreless ocean of consciousness in which I was now immersed appeared infinitely large and infinitely small at the same time, large when considered in relation to the world picture floating in it and small when considered in itself measureless without form or size, nothing and yet everything.*

He too underwent extraordinary changes which affected all his sense including that of hearing.

> *I became conscious of the fact that there had occurred an amplification and refining of auditory sensations also, as a result of which sounds heard now possessed an exotic quality and a distinctiveness that lent to music and melody a greater sweetness and to noise and clamour a more disagreeable harshness.*[3]

These changes may appear to be incomprehensible to those firmly rooted in the base chakra and the dynamics of physical living. Yet if we accept the concept of personal growth we must anticipate change. The mighty oak is quite unlike the tiny acorn. Spiritual growth precipitates change in other dimensions. The unfamiliar is often unnerving and disconcerting. The analogy of the journey is helpful, especially if we are to comprehend the higher realms where few travel. At the beginning of our journey we move with the entire human company; there is a familiarity and a shared understanding. This group moves together through the first three chakras of survival, reproduction and self-expression. However, at this point the company divides. Only a few move on; the vast majority do not.

When we think of the fifth centre in this way, we need to realise that here is a place, a state of consciousness known to even fewer people. We should not dismiss accounts which are clearly outside our own experience any more than the man in the street would dismiss the personal story of a highly trained and specialised athlete. Intrepid pioneers who have gone further than most in their journeys can be thought of as the advance scouting party sending back reports of a territory we have not yet reached.

The deities of the chakra also symbolise this new level of consciousness. Gauri Eternal as mother of the universe reminds us of our own creativity. Sadasiva has five faces and ten arms, the eye of wisdom is opened in each face. He represents omniscience, omnipresence and omnipotence. The subtle symbolism of this chakra also tells us of a significant change. We again see the elephant Airavata, first seen symbolising the stability of matter. However, we now see that the heavy collar, the sign of servitude, has been removed: we have removed the shackles which bind us to a material philosophy. We have become polarised to spirit not matter. Motoyama, our intrepid pioneer, experienced exactly this:

> *I could clearly see that I was no longer attached to this world. I became able to work freely in this world without being attached to the results of my actions. I experienced a deeply wonderful feeling of non-attachment and freedom. With this attitude, I was able to see the past, the present, and the future in the same dimension by surpassing the distinction between them.*[4]

As we move into the higher centres we encounter qualities and powers which increasingly confound the rational mind. Traditionally the awakened Vishuddi chakra is said to confer the ability to know the past, present and future, the ability to go without food and drink, to neutralise poisons outside the body and complete indestructibility. These claims defy common sense, yet the spiritual path is the quest of the uncommon traveller.

The Minor Chakras

Although we are dealing with the major chakras, there are also other minor chakras of some significance. Of these the Bindu Vishargha, the seat of nectar, is perhaps the most important. This minor chakra is located near the top of the brain towards the back of the head. This collects what is called divine nectar which then falls to the lalana centre at the epiglottis. If the Vishuddi has been sufficiently awakened, the nectar itself is purified and has the power to sustain life. There are many well-documented cases of yogis having been buried underground for forty days in states resembling suspended animation. It is said that this nectar has the power to slow down the body's metabolism and yogis buried in this way exhibit no new hair growth. Motoyama found that the Vishuddi and Bindu Visharga worked together to bring conscious control of the metabolism, respiration, food intake and digestion. Such feats are clearly outside the experience of the Western spiritual tradition yet we should not ignore the reality which they represent.

The Bindu Visharga is a centre of psychic sound. It is awakened through a sounded meditation. The breath and the sound are visualised connecting the throat and the bindu. It is said that when it is awakened a non-physical sound comprised of immeasurably subtle vibrations is heard.

If we accept that the sevenfold chakra system represents the blueprint of our being, we may eventually realise that we have many hitherto unexplored abilities, power and potentialities. As we move into the last two centres, we will be reminded of this even more firmly.

The Power of Chanting

Chanting is part of many traditions. Each sound resonates and vibrates quite differently. Sessions of group chanting have the power to shift consciousness and maintain well-being. A story is told about a doctor who was summoned to a monastery by the abbot because the monks were tired and lethargic. It transpired that the abbot had done away with the daily schedule of chanting to gain more time for other duties. However, this had achieved quite the contrary result. The monks' vigour returned when their chanting schedule was reestablished. We will use the setting of a group chant for our meditation.

Guided Meditation – The Sacred Sound

You find yourself among a great crowd in a huge hall. There is a distinct air of anticipation. You feel that you are waiting to be summoned together. As you wait you look around and see that this hall seems to hold representatives of every spiritual tradition with which you are familiar. You see Buddhists and Sikhs, Sufis and Jains. You see dark-clothed priests and monks swathed in orange. You are still gazing at the assembled crowd with some wonder when a deep gong is sounded. Its note resonates around the room and silence falls upon you all.

At the far end of the hall, double doors open. The crowd begins to move through into the hall beyond. You take your turn and finally you pass through the doors into the next hall. As you emerge into the next hall, the assembly is already being seated. You take a seat and wait.

At last everyone is seated. A deep hush falls over the assembly. Everywhere people are entering a private mood of meditation. You do the same, feeling a silent intensity in the great room. From the silence a single voice from an unseen figure strikes out a deep note. The *Aum* is sounded. Like an answering chorus the assembly replies as one. The sound fills the room, touching all extremities with its vibration. It fills your being with its vibration. It resonates within you. You feel its vibrating note shaking the very structure of your being; time seems suspended as the note rolls over and over in waves of sound. Finally the last note hangs in the air. The room is vibrant, a living tuning fork. No one moves. All are permitting the sound to work through them.

Now in the silence it seems to you that you hear an answering sound. It comes from everywhere and nowhere at the same time. You cannot detect its source, yet you hear it within you and you are content with that. You have awakened to the mysteries of sound.

Practice

- In what way may we relate the colour blue to this chakra?
- What does the name *Vishuddi* mean?
- What does the symbolism of the elephant teach us about this chakra?
- What does the attribution of *akasa* tell us?
- Which physical systems are governed by this chakra?
- What qualities might we expect when this chakra is functioning?
- Draw a circle and in it represent in some way all the activities that you associate with this chakra.

The Symbolism of the Vishuddi Chakra

The seed sound for this chakra is *Ham*.

This chakra has 16 petals coloured smoky purple.

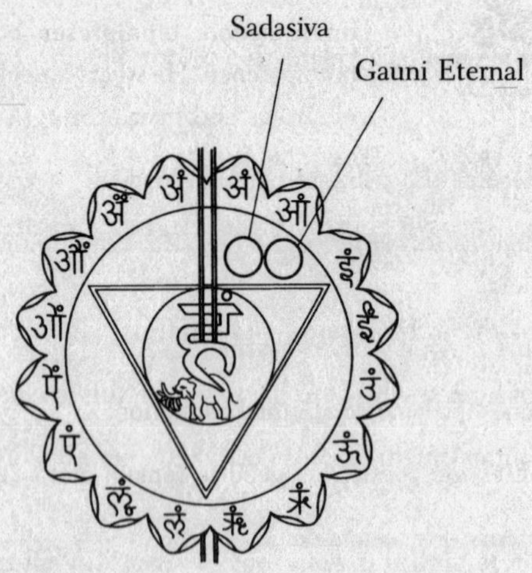

The elephant Airavata is seen without the collar which binds us to matter. This chakra is symbolised by akasa spirit.

The Akasa mandala, the circle within the triangle, represents the Gateway of Liberation.

The Deities of the Fifth Chakra

Sadasiva

Sadasiva has five faces and ten arms. In each face the eye of Wisdom is open. He symbolises omniscience; omnipresence and omnipotence. He wears a necklace of snakes and tiger skin.

The **serpent** represents the rising serpent of Wisdom.

The **trident** symbolises the unity of the physical, the etheric and causal levels of being.

The **bell** represents the function of hearing.

The **fire** represents the flame of spiritual aspiration.

The **goad** symbolises the continuing need to remain motivated.

The **sword** represents discrimination.

The **noose** reminds us against becoming trapped in the pride of knowledge.

The **dyone** or **thunderbolt** shows the awareness of power.

The **abhayamudra** gesture dispels fear.

The **battle-axe** is used to cut away outworn aspects of personality.

Gauri

Gauri is the Mother of the Universe. She is half of Lord Shiva's body. She represents eternity.

The **arrow** represents the continuing direction of our journey.

The **goad** reminds us not become too stationary and fixed in our ideas.

The **bow** symbolises the tension that must still be applied if we are to achieve our goal.

The **noose** reminds us of the traps of spiritual pride.

6

the sixth chakra

Keywords for this Chakra

Ajna Chakra
Intuition
Far-seeing
Direct-knowing
Vision
Transcendence

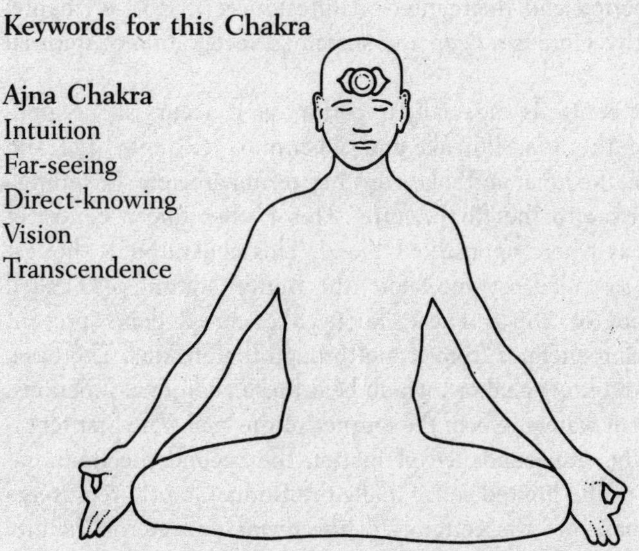

The lotus named Ajna is like the moon, beautifully white.
Verse 32, Sat-Cakra-Nirupana

The Third Eye

We are all familiar with the idea of the third eye in the forehead. This idea expresses a key function of this centre. It is the eye of the mind. The eye sees, the mind's eye knows. The name of this chakra reveals its function. *Ajna* implies both 'to know' and 'to command'. It brings quite new abilities into being. Here is an immediacy and directness which transcends the logical thought processes. Rational thinking requires deduction before conclusion. The direct knowing of the brow chakra is not a laborious conclusion but a realisation. Spiritual development gradually awakens the higher mind which functions through a direct perception. Direct knowing bypasses the ordinary mental processes. This form of consciousness can be disconcerting to those working through the concrete mind. It can appear to be extraordinary, even miraculous. This is not the fleeting and fragmented manifestation of ESP or mental telepathy. Here is a deep and sustained recognition of spiritual realities.

This centre is especially important as it occurs at the junction of the Ida, Pingala and Sushumna currents. Ida and Pingala, the lunar and solar currents, terminate here. Sushumna alone rises to the final centre. This is therefore a centre of synthesis where oppositions blend. This chakra holds the last of the so-called psychic knots, the Rudra Granthi, also called the knot of Shiva. These 'knots' like closed doors prevent ascending energies from rising through the chakras. The base, heart and brow chakras, which bear these additional functions, represent watersheds in the journey of the soul. The first represents the transcendence of matter, the second the transcendence of the limited self. Finally the Rudra Granthi represents admission into the certainty of the divine and eternal nature. These knots, which serve as doors between planes of consciousness and as locks upon certain experiences, can be opened only as inner consciousness itself forges the key.

Flights of Imagination

The sixth chakra is the first of the two head centres. It is clearly connected with the mind and the higher functions of consciousness. Whereas the previous chakras related to various physical systems, the brow chakra clearly relates to the mind, the brain and the eyes. Indeed the two petals of the chakra so like wings, are reminiscent of the two hemispheres of the brain. The central pericarp of the lotus is the place of balance where the power of the left and right hemispheres work together in harmony. Currently society places undue emphasis on the functions and qualities represented by the left brain – rationality, deduction and analysis. The qualities of the right brain – imagination, symbolic representation and synthesis – are undervalued to our cost both individually and collectively. The traditional symbol for this chakra, the two petals on either side of the centre is remarkably similar to the Egyptian winged disk which is a symbol of liberation and rebirth.

The mind can indeed be a great liberator. We even talk about 'flights of the imagination'. The imagination is not the world of make-believe and pretence which clever adults attribute to the world of children, but rather it is the image-making facility of the mind. Once again we have a tendency to devalue anything other than the world of deductive thinking. The picture-making facility relates to a higher consciousness and is far more powerful than empty words. Visualisation has always been important as a meditative technique. Metaphysicians have always understood the power of the image; creative writers and artists have always understood the powers of the internal picture.

Scientists, too, are now waking up to the potential of the visual imagination. It is now being suggested that scientists, both currently and in the past, used this ability to run tests and observe the results. The inventor Nikola Tesla by his own admission created and tested using the mind's eye. This is but one function of the Ajna chakra, the power of the imagination, that is the power to make images come alive in the mind's eye. The opening of this chakra brings a direct knowing. We see these abilities in visionaries, those who are able to make intuitive leaps of the imagination.

Those who already employ this technique in daily life, whether in meditation, creative endeavour or the field of technology, will know how the active use of the imagination expands consciousness continuously. This chakra represents the expanded mind. Those who are willing to apply a few simple principles in everyday life can easily learn to awaken and use this enriching function.

Question

- Do you use visualisation as a normal part of your daily life?

The two head chakras are related to the two major glands in the head, the pineal and the pituitary. There has been a long-standing debate over this attribution. The pineal gland is related to light, which corresponds to the crown chakra; the pituitary gland seems therefore well attributed to the Ajna chakra. The Ajna chakra functions as a command centre, the pituitary as a master gland. Its action is of great importance for health and well-being. It works with the hypothalamus to release twelve separate hormones which affect a wide range of physical functions, including uterine contractions during labour, the repair of body tissue, patterns of sleep and sexual maturation. The Ajna chakra is described by two petals, the pituitary gland is divided into two distinct parts.

The Transcendent Perspective

This centre is especially important as the process of spiritual unfoldment progresses. It is said to be quite free from karmic influences. Awakening this centre does not stir the karmic factors which traditionally beset this process. Furthermore the development of this centre enables the individual to interact with karmic factors which are both personal and of group origin. Imagine for a moment that knowledge of previous life was triggered, rising to the surface in a flood of memory. Such memories are related to the sacral chakra. However, the high vantage point of the Ajna, like a staging post near the top of a mountain, permits a transcendent perspective.

Question

- What do you understand by karma?

At its simplest, karma may be expressed as 'As ye reap so shall ye sow'. We are continuously reaping and sowing karmic seeds by words, actions, thoughts and deeds. This profound concept reminds us of the essential connection between past, present and future. It reminds us of unseen responsibilities and the debts we bear from the past.

When Hiroshi Motoyama achieved the stable awakening of the brow chakra, he was able to work directly with karmic forces. He described his own awakening in the following way:

> *My ajna chakra began to vibrate very subtly. I was completely immersed in a dark purple light while a bright white light shone from between my eyebrows. I heard a voice call me as if it were echoing in a valley. I was filled with ecstasy and a divine symbol of power was revealed to me. The state continued for one or two hours. The power to affect and alter others' karma was greatly enhanced.*[1]

He concluded that the most important aspect of awakening the Ajna chakra was 'the ability to transcend and purify karma'.

Motoyama has worked intensively with different categories of karma, which he identifies as national, racial, geographical and family-based. His intercessionary work poses many questions about the real nature of our interrelatedness. He has seen its workings at first hand in consciousness, the Ajna chakra providing this exalted perspective. We who are enmeshed in the workings of our own karma rarely have such a transcendent perspective; we are simply impelled by distant seeds planted long ago. Motoyama's experiences led him to see reincarnation as a positive evolutionary force. His practical experiences as seer and spiritual consultant led him to observe current complications and consequences which proved to be rooted in the past. It is this causal relationship which fuels the Wheel of Becoming.

The Wheel of Rebirth

The concepts of karma and reincarnation are not a part of present Western religious teachings. Yet reincarnation was taught by the early Church and was only officially abandoned at the Second Council of Constantinople in 553. The concept of reincarnation is central to Buddhism. Indeed the very concept of reincarnation is perpetually tested. Every Lama, including the Dalai Lama himself, is chosen through a stringent test; the candidate, usually a child, has to recognise those personal items formally owned in a previous incarnation. Continuity of consciousness should extend not merely from moment to moment but from incarnation to incarnation. We who perhaps find it hard to remember what happened yesterday, may find it hard to accept that conscious memory may be retained beyond death and subsequent birth. In this tradition it is not uncommon for a Lama to give indications of the future incarnation in order to help those given the task of locating the next embodiment. If such practices are outside the confines of our own spiritual traditions, we may nevertheless regard such accounts as food for serious thought.

In an unusual recent development Osel Hita Torres, the child of Spanish parents, has been formerly recognised as the new incarnation of the Lama Yeshe. The child was born in

1985, only 11 months after the death of the Lama. Lama Yeshe was a most unusual teacher who chose to work with Western students. His Western incarnation was therefore seen to be perfectly in keeping with this work. Various indications were received through both dream and oracle which made Osel one candidate among others. At 14 months he was formally tested. He had to select Lama Yeshe's mala from a collection of five and to pick out the correct bell from a total of eight. He chose correctly and soon began to show other signs which convinced everyone that the incarnate Lama Yeshe had become the incarnate Osel Hita Torres. Such are the mysteries of becoming.

Questions

- What are your feelings about the idea of reincarnation?
- Are you comfortable with the idea that you might have lived and died previously?

It is no surprise that we should find our belief system tested as we examine the qualities which belong to the higher centres. Transcendence and continuity of consciousness may not be qualities encountered every day, yet we may see them as future possibilities. Our own blueprint is still unfolding. The Ajna chakra holds deep mysteries of total being. It is close to the crown chakra and far removed from the base chakra.

The symbolism accorded to this chakra directs us to contemplate the cosmic, not the ordinary. The symbolism of human sexuality, the golden triangle of the female and the Sivalinga Itara, represent unity of a cosmic nature. The deities here are Shiva and Sakti Hakini. Shiva is not shown but represented only by the Sivalinga. Sakti Hakini has six faces and six arms representing unity. This chakra has no animal symbol. The mantra, the seed sound of this chakra is Om. Its colour is indigo, which symbolises a high vibration. This is a place of unity where apparent oppositions can be reconciled. Death and birth are transitions. Many lifetimes can be viewed from a single perspective. The essence of life-experience is distilled through karmic seeds which are carried through time. This chakra holds many mysteries. Indeed we are forced to question the very fundamentals of our existence, the meaning of life, the nature of consciousness and the passing of time.

We will use the familiar dream flying sensation to put us in touch with the consciousness represented by the Ajna chakra.

Guided Meditation – The wings of intuition

You are dreaming. In the dream anything is possible, the laws which govern the physical world do not apply. In the dream world, consciousness rules. In your dream you have found the ability to fly. Your flight is liberating and joyful. Imagine that you are airborne. You find yourself looking down upon the place where you were born. You reflect on this place and its formative influence on you. You think about your early formative influences, both people and places. You wonder if this choice was part of your own unfolding karma. You wonder if the purpose of your present life is stored away in the consciousness of the Ajna chakra. You pause and allow yourself to sink deeply into your own thoughts. You pose the time-honoured injunction, 'Know thyself'. You realise that this challenges your very notions of life and death. Is there life before birth? Is there life after death? These deep questions fill your mind as you hover in your mind's eye over the place of your birth.

You wonder if there have been other birth-places for you. All is stored within consciousness, and memories – no matter how deep or distant – can surface when the time is right. Your consciousness is free in this moment. Allow your flight body to travel wherever it wills. You experience the sensation of movement. The movement stops. In your mind's eye you hover above another birthplace. Perhaps you can make out some features of time and place. You may reflect upon this place, allowing your deep intuitive sense to guide your thoughts and feelings. Finally your mind's eye begins to close. As the images begin to fade, you return to waking consciousness with many thoughts, feelings and questions. Perhaps you have truly touched the deep mystery of the Ajna chakra.

Practice

- In what way may we relate the colour indigo to this chakra?
- What does the name *Ajna* mean?
- What does the absence of animal and elemental symbolism tell us about this chakra?
- What does the symbolism of the downward-pointing triangle teach us about this chakra?
- Which physical systems are governed by this chakra?
- What qualities might we expect if this chakra is functioning?
- Draw a circle and in it represent in some way all the activities that you associate with this chakra.

The Symbolism of the Ajna Chakra

The quarter moon barely visible reminds us that this energy is most subtle.

The mantra for this chakra is *Om*.

The two white petals are like wings.

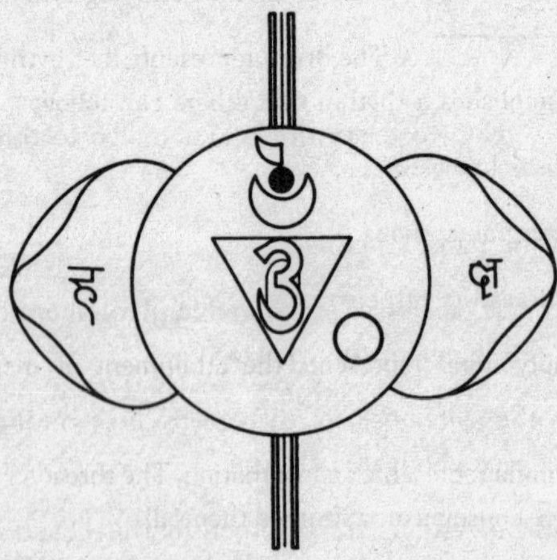

The bindu, the golden spot, represents essential energy from which we come and return.

The golden triangle represents the Feminine Power. It contains the Sivalinga. Together they express unity and harmony. The triangle also represents the function of the three separate currents, Ida, Pingala and Sushumna.

The Deities of the Sixth Chakra

Sakti Hakini

Sakti Hakini has six faces and six arms. Sakti Hakini represents both the god and goddesses of this chakra, another unifying symbol.

The **drum** represents the rhythm of life. The Adept establishes a rhythm that others can follow.

The **book** symbolises knowledge.

The **varada** gesture grants boons.

The **abhayamudra** gesture dispels fear.

The **skull** as empty mind represents the attainment of mental powers.

Each bead on the **mala** represents an incarnation. The thread which is the continuity of consciousness unifies them all.

7

the seventh chakra

Keywords for this Chakra

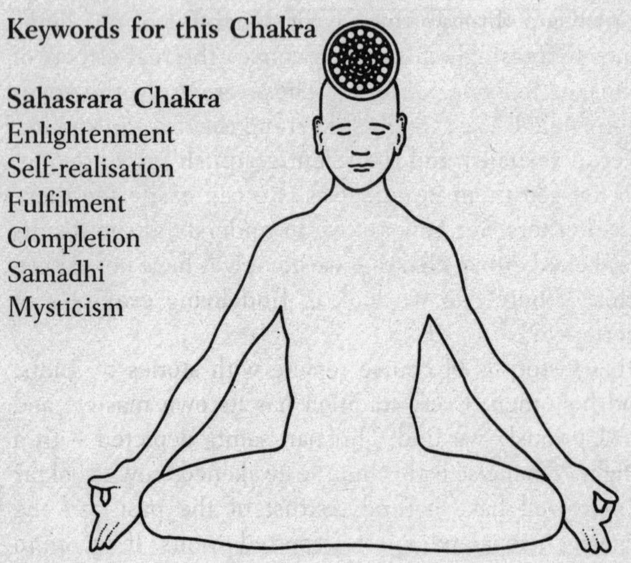

Sahasrara Chakra
Enlightenment
Self-realisation
Fulfilment
Completion
Samadhi
Mysticism

Wise men describe it as the abode of Vishnu, and righteous men speak of it as the ineffable place of knowledge of the Atma, or the Place of Liberation.

Verse 49, Sat-Cakra-Nirupana

The Crown of Light

The chakra at the top of the head is called the crown. This simple title tells us a great deal. Here is our crowning achievement, the thousandfold crown, the Sahasrara chakra. We began our journey at the base chakra with its four petals and red attribution. We have now reached the place of a thousand petals which signify qualities without number. This chakra is attributed to the colour violet. We have travelled from simplicity to complexity, from instinct to transcendence. We have traversed the rainbow. We have moved from red to violet, from matter to spirit. The goal represented by the Sahasrara chakra is in fact our return to the source. Our journey has been the Way of Return.

As we rise up through the cosmic blueprint of our being it becomes increasingly difficult to convey the real effects of the expansion in consciousness. These are truly the roads less well travelled. We can all understand the drive to survive, the power in sexuality and the relentless push for autonomy. If we do not see them in ourselves, we can easily see these qualities in others. Yet how are we to understand the results of the awakened crown chakra if we ourselves have not experienced this. Where can we look to find living examples of this experience?

Spiritual history is of course replete with stories of saints, sages and holy men. Every tradition has its own masters and teachers. Curiously we find Christian saints depicted with a shining light. What else is this but the awakened crown chakra? Yet we may well have natural distrust of the past and the centuries which separate us from reported events. If we are to understand the place of enlightenment in human history, we need to see it as an eternal event, not a relic of history.

Malcolm Muggeridge reports a curious tale about Mother Theresa, a contemporary saint in the Christian tradition. He was preparing to film her in a cathedral, the dim lighting of which was insufficient for a film shoot. He expressed the concerns of the camera crew but he went ahead as no other options were available to him. Instead of the poor quality he had expected, the film was perfect. He was mystified by this and acknowledged that a minor miracle had occurred. He came to believe that they were filming by the living light of a contemporary holy person. It is also curious that the pineal gland which responds to the crown chakra is in some way affected by light. The Tibetan also talks about the 'light in the head'. This is subjectively experienced as an inner light: 'Students frequently speak of a diffused light or glow . . . later they may speak of seeing what appears to be like a sun in the head.'[1]

Gopi Krishna experienced this too: 'It was not difficult to understand that, without my being aware of it, an extraordinary change had taken place in the now luminous cognitive centre of my brain and that the fascinating lustre, which I perceived around every object, was not a figment of my fancy nor was it possessed by the objects, but a projection of my own internal radiance.'[2] He further concluded 'that by virtue of the evolutionary processes still going on in the human body, a high-powered conscious centre is being evolved by nature in the human brain at a place near the crown of the head built of exceptionally sensitive brain tissue.'[3] We also use the term 'enlightened' to refer to the awakened being. Perhaps this term has a literal as well as a symbolic meaning.

Question

- What does the term 'enlightenment' mean to you?

The Experience of Unity

At these levels of awakened consciousness, we should expect the unexpected. We are not dealing with the familiar and the ordinary but rather the unfamiliar and the extraordinary. Such occurrences are unusual only because those who have attained this level of spiritual realisation are numerically few. By definition such events upset our ordinary view of what can and cannot happen. We are forced to rethink our whole philosophical framework. Rather than expand our view of reality to incorporate the miraculous, it is so much easier to maintain the comfortable status quo of our own world view and exclude the unusual as inexplicable aberrations. When we do this both personally and as a group we hold onto the present at the expense of the future. We simply restrict the possibility of growth by imposing a tight grip on our structure of reality.

Opening up at these higher levels of consciousness can only take place when a genuine openness of mind exists. The closed mind will never permit a personal experience to take hold. Philosophical frameworks of reality are important as tools, but they should never become prisons. I remember overhearing a learned gentleman ticking off a medium by telling her that such things were entirely fabricated, being totally impossible as Wittgenstein had so clearly shown through his philosophical arguments. I smiled and went on my way musing on who was the poorer, the philosopher or the medium! A philosophical or metaphysical framework must provide for the possibility of growth if it is to be of any service to the individual. If the intellectual construct is closed, it will only imprison and indeed destroy in the long term. Experience is truly the best and only teacher, especially in matters spiritual. The framework can only provide recognisable landmarks, the experience shows us the landscape.

These higher levels are intensely personal and can only be experienced through both courage and devotion. Theory is swept away by the power of the passionate experience. Intellectual learning is a thing of the past as bliss, rapture and ecstasy overwhelm in the moment. As women attempt to prepare themselves for childbirth, the event supersedes all preparation and stamps the event with a mark which is personal and beyond everything else. So, travellers at these levels of consciousness need to be prepared in mind, heart and spirit, yet in truth no preparation is adequate for the birth of your divine self.

Question

- Do you believe in the reality of mystical states of consciousness?

These states are recognised by all long-established spiritual traditions. The terminology may differ but the experiences are essentially the same. Whether called *samadhi* or mystical union, such intense states share common characteristics. They are usually transient and convey a sense of timelessness. There is a sense of passivity in which the individual feels a degree of surrender to the experience. The personal ego feels insubstantial and unreal by comparison. There is an overwhelming sense of the unity of all life within the framework of an experience which speaks through the emotions but defies intellectual explanation. Yet despite the inevitable brevity of the episode, its intensity conveys a deep and lasting knowledge. This is the mystical experience.

The Thousandfold Mystery

The crown chakra holds many mysteries for the individual and for humanity as a whole. We live at an important time. In the past, mystical consciousness has indeed been treated as a form of aberrant and bizarre event. There is little doubt in my mind that in the age to come, we will understand that it is both normal and beneficial. Gopi Krishna himself regarded the force represented by the seven chakras as being a positive evolutionary force. The number of mystical people in the world will surely increase. There was truly a time when mystical consciousness was only brought to birth as part of an enclosed spiritual tradition. Monasteries, communities, ashrams, convents and temples have without a doubt shielded many a mystic from the world. With the accessibility of spiritual knowledge and the widespread appearance of a teaching generation, these higher levels are being awakened by devoted and truly spiritual people who live not behind closed walls but in the community at large.

Question

- Are you sufficiently motivated to take up the long preparatory period required to precipitate a transcendental experience?

The crown chakra is of such importance that it is often described as being quite different from the first six chakras. Accordingly the crown chakra has no mantra. It is quite beyond descriptions, which by nature can only limit. It confers transcendence. It is a unique centre, the Abode of Shiva. It is the goal of the ascended Kundalini which resides sleeping within the base chakra. Spiritual teachers are often curiously and deliberately silent about this centre. The chakras are sometimes described as being six in number to emphasise this distinction.

The crown chakra is described through some symbols however: 'This lotus, lustrous and whiter than the full moon, has its head turned downwards, it charms. Its clustered filaments are tinged with the colour of the young sun.[4] At the pericarp or centre of the lotus, we find the mandalas of Surya, the sun and Candra, the moon. Within the Candra mandala is a triangle 'shining like lightning and inside this again shines the Great Void which is served in secret by all the Suras'. The concept of the void may be foreign, even frightening to the Western mind. The Great Void is not an empty space; there can be no such thing but potentiality. Such ideas are difficult if not impossible to conceptualise, but then so are the ideas of contemporary physics. We are, however, quite happy to accept the reality of subatomic particles, black holes and dark matter. Matter and spirit possess many mysteries.

Question

- Do you use your mind to think about material or spiritual realities?

The crown chakra holds the unfathomable mystery which we cannot hope to grasp except through analogy and second-hand experience. Motoyama's experience took place in the following way during a session of deep meditation:

> *A shining golden light began to enter and leave my body through the top of my head and I felt as if the top of my head protruded ten to twenty centimetres. In the astral but not physical dimension, I saw what looked like the head of Buddha, shimmering purple and blue, resting on the top of my own head. There was a golden-white light flowing in and out through the gate on the top of the Buddha's crown. Gradually I lost the sensation of my body, but I held a clear awareness of consciousness and super-consciousness . . . I was able to hear a powerful but very tender voice resounding throughout the universe. I realised spontaneously my mission in my previous lives, my spiritual state and many other things. After the awakening of the sahasrara chakra, the abilities that had come through the awakening of the lower chakras became stronger. I received the following abilities, the ability to enter and affect the bodies of others; the ability to extend my existence and to include others within it; the ability to work freely, transcending karma and the restrictions of the body, and the ability to be granted union with the divine power.*[5]

The extraordinary abilities and transcendental mystical states must make us question any model of reality which excludes such possibilities. We have lived too long in a philosophical straightjacket which has neatly but lethally divided spirit from matter. We have lived too long in the shadow of fear-driven dogma and crushing materialism. Spiritual awakening is about personal liberation and the quest for reality. Ultimately it is about experience not dogma. The many mysteries of the crown chakra beckon like a lighthouse in the darkness unfailingly drawing us home.

This chakra represents the culmination of the spiritual journey, but this is not to say that the journey is over. We will use a theme that is familiar from both mythology and history to represent this crowning moment. In the Tibetan Tantric tradition, the student is actually crowned, 'raised from the level of an infant to a king or queen' in the *abhiseka* ceremony which presents the student formally with the experience of transmission. The crown remains a powerful spiritual symbol even in an age of democracy.

Guided Meditation – The Coronation

Imagine that you once set out on a journey. It began so long ago that you do not remember the beginning. Yet your mind contains many memories for you have indeed travelled through every experience. Each experience has taught you something. You carry the quintessence of your travels with the very fibre of your being.

You begin to recall your many memories but they crowd in upon you in their irrelevance. You have walked many paths, dwelt in many civilisations, peered from beneath many a disguise, adopted many a new body, passed many times through the tunnel of change in consciousness.

And now something new beckons, your inner voice bids you take stock of your long journey in consciousness. As you do so you find yourself beginning to rise, floating up in the body of light which you have created from your words, deeds and actions. You wonder where you are travelling, no sooner do you wonder than you arrive.

You stand at the centre of a vast circular hall. You wear a long cloak which covers you from head to foot. The hall is filled with a clear and brilliant light which is filtered through seven great windows. It is filled with many people. At first you wonder who they are and why they are here. You realise that these are all the people whose lives have intertwined with yours as you have journeyed from life to life. Beaming faces smile at you. You instantly recognise some faces; others are less familiar but not forgotten.

The crowds part to reveal a path leading towards a raised dais at the far end. You realise that this path is cleared for you. So you walk and ascend the stairs from where you can see all of the assembly, and they can see you. You stand wondering what is to happen. The hall is hushed. A gentle voice speaks on the silence: 'Stand forward and be recognised in this place.' You step forward and as you do so, the cloak falls from your shoulders and you stand forth as a being of light, radiant and scintillating. You shimmer with an inner light which is entirely your own. You are amazed at this mystery for you have glimpsed the reality of your own being.

As you survey the assembly you see that a young child is now approaching the staircase. The child carries a cushion and on it you see a crown. The child stands before you and offers up the crown. You know that you have come to be crowned. No other may do this but yourself. You lift the crown over your head, holding it suspended momentarily. It is a crown composed of a thousand precious petals.

You place the crown upon your head and as you do so it completely vanishes from sight. In its place a halo of living light shines out, and tongues of living fire lick the air. The same soft voice speaks out: 'You are recognised in this place. I offer you a choice. You may journey to destinations unknown and places new, or you may return to carry those who cannot carry themselves and to show light to those who seek it.'

You make your decision then cloak yourself once more. You pick up your cloak and place it about yourself. Your brilliant light is concealed. The surroundings fade and you return once more to a familiar place. Your new journey now begins.

Practice

- In what way may we relate the colour violet to this chakra?
- What does the name *Sahasrara* mean?
- What do we learn from the absence of animal and elemental symbols?
- What does the symbolism of the Great Void teach us?
- Which physical systems are governed by this chakra?
- What qualities might we expect if this chakra is functioning?
- Draw a circle and in it represent in some way all the activities that you associate with this chakra.

The Symbolism of the Symbolism of the Seventh Chakra

The pericarp of the lotus contains the mandalas of sun and moon and the bindu without attributes.

The thousand petals now turn downwards.

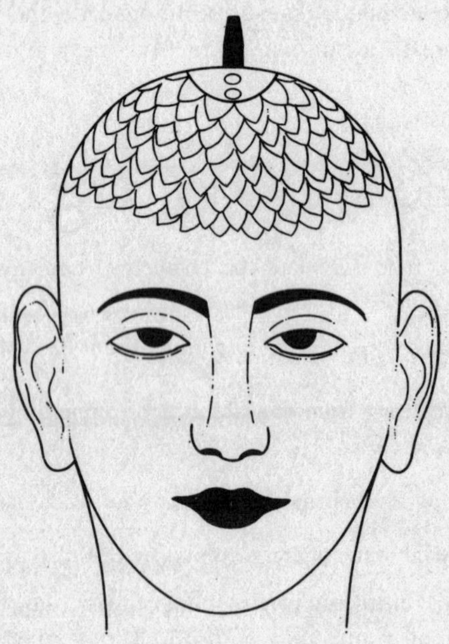

'I meditate on the guru in the lotus of a thousand petals, which is radiant like the cool rays of the full moon, whose lotus hands make the gestures which grant blessings and dispel fear. His raiment, garland, and perfumes, are ever fresh and pure.'

Introductory Verse: Paduka-Pancaka

8

the rainbow light

Awakening the chakras is a very important event in man's evolution.

Swami Satyananda Saraswati

The preceding chapters have provided you with no more than a brief outline; there is, of course, a world of difference between theory and practice. When considering chakra work, we should always be mindful of traditional caution. Times may have changed radically, the human psyche, however, changes little.

We should never forget that chakra awakening is spiritual awakening. As the blueprint unfolds, so we are greatly changed. Personal change is unavoidable and inevitable. Chakra awakening implies personal responsibility; chakra awakening demands commitment; chakra awakening precipitates change. If you are willing to take responsibility, if you have long-term commitment, if you are willing to face change, you may discover the difference between theory and practice.

The Unity of The Chakra System

The image of the rainbow is often connected with the chakras; as we have already seen, each of the seven colours is attributed to one of the chakras. This sevenfold light also reminds us of the essential unity of the chakra system. We divide the one into the seven for our own convenience and intellectual understanding; in reality it is less simple to make this artificial distinction.

There is a deep interrelationship between mind, body and spirit. There is a deep interrelationship between thought, energy and matter. Change in one chakra may flow into another chakra, even when these secondary results are not immediately apparent. There are also particular polarities between certain chakras which set up dynamic relationships. For instance the Ajna chakra can be stimulated by passing energy through the spine from the base chakra. There is also a deep relationship between the sacral chakra, which represents reproductive creativity, and the throat chakra, which represents personal creativity. These relationships should remind us that it is always a mistake to treat the seven chakras as being separate. It is practically impossible for change within one chakra not to affect another, even when this is not immediately apparent. The chakras are switches upon the same circuit. This essential unity directly affects the way in which individuals experience awakening through the chakras. We cannot conclude our brief survey of the rainbow light without referring to the potent *kundalini* experience, when energy moves through all the chakras simultaneously, using the spine as its channel. Spiritual awakening often takes the form of a *kundalini* experience.

Dynamics of Spiritual Growth

There are many approaches to chakra work and ultimately to *kundalini* itself. We are now immersed in metaphysical activity of all kinds. The spiritual retreat has all but vanished; the weekend workshop now reigns supreme. In this new and increasingly spiritualised atmosphere, it is important that we should be aware of the interconnections between all manifestations of spiritual growth. Intense input of a spiritual nature, whether through meditation, healing or devotion, will create direct change in the personal energies. We can affect the chakra blueprint unintentionally. We need to understand the dynamics of spiritual growth; we need to be familiar with situations which might act as triggers for chakra awakening. *Forewarned is forearmed.*

Case Studies

Awakening through the chakras may take many forms; traditional practices such as yoga and meditation are now being supplemented through contemporary and experimental approaches. The actual experience of awakening may also take many forms. It is often, though not always, dramatic. Case histories can be very helpful and show the wide range of possible encounters. There are of course many ways of awakening through the chakras; every case is quite personal. Yet we may, for our own convenience, loosely group certain types of awakening.

Spontaneous Awakening

Spontaneous awakening is a rare event; it is the mark of a spiritualised soul. If the event is recognised for what it is, difficulties can be averted. Those who go on to become significant spiritual teachers in adult life commonly experience this form of awakening in early life. The experience of Swami Satyananda Saraswati is typical of such awakenings which apparently appear quite unbidden. His story is recounted in *Kundalini Tantra*[1].

When I was six years old, I had a spontaneous spiritual experience during which I became completely unaware of my body for quite a long time. Again when I was ten the same thing happened, but this time I was old enough to think and rationalise, and I told my father about it.

My father had a great regard for the Vedas and for his guru. One day this guru happened to visit my native town, so my father took me to him and asked his advice about me. The sage told him that I had had a spiritual experience and therefore should be instructed to lead a spiritual life. My father obeyed the guru and arranged for me to be trained accordingly; thus at an early age I was dedicated to the spiritual quest.

The average person is highly unlikely to experience awakening in this form. Nevertheless it forms a significant category of its own and many recognised spiritual leaders follow this pattern.

Disciplined Awakening

The traditional avenues of awakening to spiritual reality stress the development of the whole person. In the East, yoga offers a gradual and organic system of change and development. Kundalini yoga deals exclusively with the sevenfold chakra blueprint through dynamic movement, breathing and mantra. In the West, Kabbala awakens the qualities represented by the chakras through symbolism and meditation. Both systems offer a long-term path of discipline and developing self-awareness. Within such systems, awakening through the chakra blueprint happens gradually at an individual pace. There is a great deal to be said for the stability of a tradition and the experience of a teacher. It is quite possible to awaken during private practice or to experience this within a large group, where of course the spiritual energies are intensified. The following account appears in *Kundalini, Evolution and Enlightenment*[2]. It reports an experience which took place during a Yoga convocation. The writer had already studied yoga for five years at the time. His experience began during a group chanted meditation.

> *I began to realise that something unusual was happening to me. The first thing I noticed was a wave of euphoria softly permeating my being. I felt intensely happy. I didn't know the reason for the wonderful feeling but I determined to relax and enjoy it. Suddenly surges of energy-like electrical changes streaked up my spine. These gradually evolved into a steady current of hot energy flowing from the tip of my spine to the top of my head. Brilliant colours swirled inside my head; I thought I would burst with happiness . . . Suddenly the whole thing stopped as abruptly as it had begun, the energy inside me subsided and the room quietened.*

Yoga has proved to be the vehicle for awakening throughout the centuries. Contemporary serious students may well experience the rising of Kundalini despite the fact that in the West, yoga has become fragmented. The postures have become divorced from the metaphysical philosophy. Mere callisthenics alone will never create the spiritual dynamic required to fuel a deep transformation. Spiritual awakening is a multi-level experience; it is not confined to the body alone.

Precipitate Awakening

The deep connections between many forms of spiritual activity mean that under certain circumstances it is possible to activate chakra energies unexpectedly. This can bring its own problems. When awakening is precipitate, the individual is quite unprepared for the effects. A considerable period of readjustment may be required. Such awakening is unusual, though not uncommon by any means. It takes place when a highly sensitive person is exposed to a particular trigger which may be quite innocuous. It can also take place through the intervention of a second individual who exploits psychic vulnerability. Highly sensitised individuals usually conceal a spiritual potency which is dormant. Under these circumstances, the eruption of a perfectly ordinary life is often quite unwelcome and troublesome. Characteristically, the individual is then forced to undertake the quest for understanding. Ironically this short-term disruption often proves in the long term to be a deep and enriching fulfilment. Such cases are quite individual and unusual. It is therefore not possible to provide a typical case history.

Unexpected Awakening

Spiritual practices such as meditation clearly have the power to awaken. Curiously, individuals are often caught unprepared as Kundalini unexpectedly awakens in response to the changes created through meditation. In fact, such an effect should come as no surprise. However, as meditation practice is not specifically designed to bring this effect about, students are often ill-prepared for the eventuality.

From the wide range of personal testaments, it is evident that all meditation systems have the potential to activate the deep chakra blueprint. There is often a time-lapse of several years between taking up regular meditation practice and the personal Kundalini experience. The following is a fairly typical example. It is reported in *The Kundalini Experience*.

> *In the spring of 1966 I was awakened with such a quantum leap of subtle energy in my body that I was unable to sleep for over two months. I knew nothing about Kundalini at that time; it was others who subsequently recognised what was happening to me as a Kundalini awakening. My experience was sudden, unexpected and undeniable. It was not easy – all the more since no one around me knew of such things. I often felt expanded, joyful and extremely nourished spiritually, especially when I was alone. In 1963 I had started Zen meditation and I believe it was largely my meditation practice that led to the awakening.*

There can be no doubt of the validity and power of such testaments. These witnesses have experienced deep and profound shifts in the blueprint of being which is encapsulated within the sevenfold chakras, the rainbow light.

The Spiritual Quest

We may not feel able to undertake the quest with single-minded zeal but we can at least know that it is there for us when we are ready. The reality of such experiences should also remind us why knowledge of the chakras was once secret.

This body of knowledge will still only speak to the few; it is truly esoteric. Some will be content to absorb this information at an intellectual level, but a still smaller group will be fired by a deep need for transcendence. They will set out on the personal quest without a further thought. Such is the nature of this work. Those who read with understanding are preparing to quest in the future. To those who are ready to quest, I can only say that there is great truth in the old statement *When the student is ready, the teacher will appear*.

If you feel moved to seek out a teacher, I wish you well. In truth, the quest has to be enacted at all levels; if you did not quest you would not value its treasure. If you have a serious commitment to your own awakening through the chakras, I offer you a meditation and a ceremonial beginning in Appendix I at the end of this book. You may affirm your intent through these forms. Intent is of great importance as it sets the tone for the future. If you take your chakra awakening seriously, you will be given the appropriate opportunities; if you see chakra work as a flippant excursion into the curious, you will also draw appropriate circumstances to yourself.

conclusion

We have touched upon the deep and fundamental issues of the human condition. We have heard testimony both spiritual and scientific. We have wondered about the mysterious Kundalini. We have posed many questions. We have raised many more, for this is not an area for easy answers and glib solutions. We should not deceive ourselves; we have merely touched the surface of a vast and once hidden tradition.

Let us give the last word to Dr Hiroshi Motoyama, whose personal testament has enriched our armchair journey. As Shinto priest and scientist, he represents the marriage of two seemingly disparate disciplines. His success credits both disciplines and shows us the way forwards. He believes firmly that the way forward lies with both the scientific and the spiritual: 'I feel that the continuation of research into the nature of psi energy, by many others as well as myself, will lead to considerable changes in our views of matter, of mind and body, of human beings, and the whole word.'[1] Let us see if he is right in his assumption. Ask yourself, have your views about matter, the mind, the body, the human being and the whole world been changed by this book?

Naomi Ozaniec is currently researching the Kundalini experience. If you would like to share any personal accounts, please write to:

BCM Box 6812
London
WC1N 3XX
England

Appendix 1
meditation and affirmation

The Rainbow Meditation

Create a space in the mind. Become aware of your breathing. When you are ready, commence the visualised meditation in the following way.

Place your attention at the base of the spine. Use your imaginative mind to create a sphere of white light here. This represents the Muladhara chakra; this represents your connection to the Earth. You may allow yourself to think about the Earth in any way you wish.

While holding the sphere of Muladhara in your mind, place your attention over the lower abdomen. Create a sphere of white light here. This represents the Svadisthana chakra; this represents your connection to other people. You may allow yourself to think about the other people in your life.

While holding the spheres of Muladhara and Svadisthana in your mind, place your attention over the centre of the belly. Create a sphere of white light here. This represents the Manipura chakra; this symbolises your place of self determination. You may allow yourself to think about your own direction and drive in life.

While holding the spheres of Muladhara, Svadisthana, and Manipura, place your attention at the level of the heart. Create a sphere of white light here. This represents the Anahata chakra; this symbolises your ability to love freely and with compassion. You may dwell here upon the suffering of humanity.

While holding the spheres of Muladhara, Svadisthana, Manipura and Anahata, place your attention at the throat. Create a sphere of white light here. This represents the Vishuddi chakra; this symbolises your creativity and expression. You may dwell upon the ways in which you express yourself.

While holding the spheres of Muladhara, Svadisthana, Manipura, Anahata and Vishuddi, place your attention in the space between the eyebrows. Create a sphere of white light here. This represents the Ajna chakra; this symbolises the place of dreams and visions. You may dwell upon your own capacity to dream.

While holding the spheres of Muladhara, Svadisthana, Manipura, Anahata, Vishuddi and Ajna, place your attention to the point just above the top of your head. Create a sphere of white light here. This is the place of your own cosmic force and divine nature; this represents the Sahasrara chakra. You may dwell upon what you understand by this.

Spend a minimum of a single session establishing each sphere before moving on the next. At the end of each daily session when you have built one sphere, be sure to dismantle it before you close the meditation session. It does not matter how long it takes you to build the exercise to completion. When you have built all seven spheres, go on to the next phase, *The fountain*. Only move on to *The fountain* when you can hold all seven spheres in your mind simultaneously.

The Fountain

Turn your attention to the space just below the feet. On an in-breath, imagine white light pouring up through the legs into the base chakra. This light rises up from the base creating a column of white light. Allow this light to rise up through each of the spheres. When the light reaches the crown chakra above the head, on an out-breath allow it to cascade over the body descending downwards. Visualise the light pouring back into the earth.

Repeat this three times. When this is finished, dismantle the process as in *The rainbow* meditation. When you are confident in both *The rainbow* and *The fountain* you might wish to make a deeper commitment by establishing the ceremony of the rainbow light. The following ceremony *The living rainbow* is short and simple. It is in essence an enacted affirmation.

The Living Rainbow

Light candle

I light the candle.
The light shines out.
The candle is transformed.
The light is sevenfold.
I receive the light.

I establish the living rainbow, the mirror of my inner being.

Sit and perform *The rainbow meditation* and *The fountain*

May the power and the mystery sustain me.
May the sevenfold wisdom be awakened within me.
May the sevenfold light glow within me.
May the sevenfold lotus grace me.
May I awaken to my sevenfold heritage.

My work is begun, I open the lotus.
My work is ended, I depart in peace.
My work in the world is transformed.

Extinguish candle

Appendix 2
table of correspondences

SANSKRIT NAME Muladahara
LOCATION Base of spine
GLAND Adrenals
COLOUR Red
PETALS 4

ELEMENT Earth
ANIMAL Elephant
SENSE Smell
MANTRA Lam

SANSKRIT NAME Svadisthana
LOCATION Genitals
GLAND Testes/ovaries
COLOUR Orange
PETALS 6

ELEMENT Water
ANIMAL Makara
SENSE Taste
MANTRA Vam

SANSKRIT NAME Manipura
LOCATION Solar plexus
GLAND Pancreas
COLOUR Yellow
PETALS 10

ELEMENT Fire
ANIMAL Ram
SENSE Sight
MANTRA Ram

SANSKRIT NAME Anahata
LOCATION Heart
GLAND Thymus
COLOUR Green
PETALS 12

ELEMENT Air
ANIMAL Gazelle
SENSE Touch
MANTRA Yam

SANSKRIT NAME Vishuddi
LOCATION Throat
GLAND Thyroid
COLOUR Blue
PETALS 16
ELEMENT Akasa
ANIMAL Elephant
SENSE Hearing
MANTRA Ham

SANSKRIT NAME Ajna
LOCATION Brow
GLAND Pituitary
COLOUR Indigo
PETALS 2
ELEMENT None
ANIMAL None
SENSE None
MANTRA Om

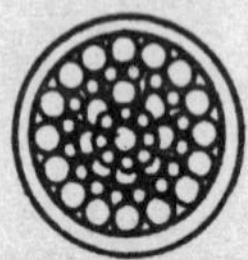

SANSKRIT NAME Sahasrara
LOCATION Crown of head
GLAND Pineal
COLOUR Violet
PETALS 1000
ELEMENT None
ANIMAL None
SENSE None
MANTRA None

glossary

Apana one of the five types of prana.
Ashram a spiritual community.
Aum a universal mantra.

Bindu a dot or point often at the centre of a mandala.
Bindu visharga the minor but important chakra in the head.

Caduceus the wand of Hermes.

Granthi (of Brahma, of Vishnu, and of Shiva or Rudra) a psychic knot found within three chakras.

Ida the lunar current.

Kalpa tree the wish-fulfilling tree, the minor centre within the heart chakra.
Kirlian photography electrical discharge photography.
Kundalini the power which rises from the base chakra to the crown.

Makara the mythical creature symbolising the powers of the Svadisthana chakra.
Mala a rosary.
Mantra a sounded meditation.

Pingala the solar current.

Prana the subtle life-energy.
Prana Vidya the knowledge of prana.
Pranayama the science of the applied breath.
Privithi the yantra of earth.

Samana one of the five types of prana.
Sushumna the current which rises through the spine from the base chakra to the crown chakra.

Tibetan, The the spiritual teacher behind the collected works of Alice Bailey.
Tumo the generation of psychic heat.

Usana one of the five forms of prana.
Uyana one of the five forms of prana.

Yantra a geometric design used as a focus for meditation.

notes

Introduction

1. Motoyama, *The Theories of the Chakras*, p.274.

Chapter 2 – The Second Chakra

1. Motoyama, p.242.

Chapter 3 – The Third Chakra

1. Motoyama, p.246.

Chapter 4 – The Fourth Chakra

1. Alice Bailey, *A Treatise on White Magic*, p.197.
2. Gopi Krishna, *Kundalini*, p.210.
3. Mason and Laing, *Sathya Sai Baba*, p.23.
4. *Caduceus*, Issue 23, 'Sounds from the Source'.

Chapter 5 – The Fifth Chakra

1. Motoyama, p.251.
2. Bailey, p.480.
3. Krishna, p.145.
4. Motoyama, p.251.

Chapter 6 – The Sixth Chakra

1. Motoyama, p.253.

Chapter 7 – The Seventh Chakra

1. Bailey, p.107.

2. Krishna, p.145.
3. Krishna, p.163.
4. Arthur Avalon (Sir John Woodroffe), *The Serpent Power*, p.419.
5. Motoyama, p.254.

Chapter 8 – The Rainbow Light

1. *Kundalini Tantra*, p.1.
2. John White, *Kundalini, Evolution and Enlightenment*, p.184.
3. Lee Sannella, *The Kundalini Experience*, p.83.

Conclusion

1. Motoyama, p.279.

further reading

Anodea, Judith, *Wheels of Life*, Llewellyn Books, 1987

Avalon, Arthur (Sir John Woodroffe), *The Serpent Power*, Luzac, 1919

Bailey, Alice, *A Treatise on White Magic*, Lucis Press, 1974

Brennan, Barbara, *Hands of Light*, Bantam Books, 1988

Henderson, Angela, 'Sounds from the Source' in *Caduceus* (23), 1994

Krishna, P., Gopi, R., *Kundalini – The Evolutionary Energy in Man*, Shambhala, 1985

Mason, and Laing, *Sathya Sai Baba*, Pilgrim Books, 1982

Motoyama, Hiroshi, *Theories of the Chakras*, Quest Books, 1981

Ozaniec, Naomi, *The Elements of the Chakras*, Element Books, 1990

Reed, Michael, *Acu Yoga*, Gach, Japan Publications Inc., 1981

Sannella, Lee, *The Kundalini Experience*, Integral Publishing, 1987

Sherwood, Kcith, *Chakra Thcrapy*, Llewellyn Books, 1988

White, John (Editor), *Kundalini, Evolution and Enlightenment*, Paragon House, 1990